Guardians at Work: A Study of Police Officers' Lives

ElioEndless

PREFACE

Hey there, "wave"! How's it going? I'm your friendly neighborhood book editor, here to tell you about this amazing book that just landed on our shelves. It's a gem that our awesome publishing company has brought to life. Now, as part of my job, I get to dive into countless books, and I must say, this one is an absolute delight. No need for any unnecessary delay, let me give you a sneak peek into what makes it so worthwhile. Are you ready? Let's jump right in with the introductionThe vital role of human resources in contributing to a country's economic development is undeniable. Economic progress hinges on the effective utilization of a nation's physical resources by its labor force and other forms of manpower to fully harness the country's production potential. Within the service sector, human resources emerge as the most significant contributor to the Indian economy.For most adults, the domains of work and life hold utmost importance. Regardless of one's profession, achieving a balance between work and life is an imperative challenge faced by all employees. Work-life balance is not only essential for the workforce but also crucial for the organization itself. When employees successfully strike a balance between their work and personal lives, it becomes evident in their performance and effectiveness in both spheres—work and life. The right equilibrium between work and life plays a pivotal role in attaining both personal and organizational goals. Moreover, work-life balance significantly influences employees' attitudes towards their organization and their overall satisfaction with their lives.

In recent decades, sweeping changes in the social, religious, political, and economic landscape have spurred a rapid increase in the number of women entering the paid labor force in India and elsewhere. The rise in women's literacy rates in India has resulted in a demographic shift, marked by a growing number of women in the workforce. In the 21st century, a substantial portion of women has been engaged in various fields. According to the latest census data from 2011, 25.6% of women in India actively participate in the workforce. The surge in nuclear and dual-earner families has placed significant pressure on both men and women to effectively manage their work and family responsibilities.

The profession of policing presents a challenging, and at times, outright hostile work environment for both women and men officers. Achieving work-life balance poses a critical issue for police personnel. Policing stands out as one of the occupations characterized by a high level of stress. The duties of police constables encompass a wide array of responsibilities, including law enforcement, peacekeeping, protection of individuals and property, and investigative work.

To Dad, Mom, and my supportive colleagues,Your love, guidance, and unwavering support have been the driving force behind my journey as a writer. Thank you for believing in me and encouraging me to pursue my dreams. Your presence in my life has made all the difference.

With heartfelt gratitude,

ELIO.E

For more information or to book an event, please contact: global.publishers@elioendless.com
Website: https://elioendless.com

Book design by Kai
Cover design by Tyson

Paperback ISBN:
ebook ISBN:

⎣⎡⎦ ElioEndless

ACKNOWLEDGMENTS

I would like to take this opportunity to extend my heartfelt thanks to all the individuals who have played a significant role in the creation of this non-fiction book. Your unwavering support, valuable advice, and constant encouragement have been invaluable throughout this journey. I am deeply grateful to those who have provided me with aspirational direction, constructive criticism, and kind advice. Your feedback has been instrumental in shaping the content and direction of this book. I genuinely appreciate your candid insights into my project.I am particularly grateful for the exceptional assistance of Mr. Jaffer and Mrs. Sameena at Endless Publishers. Their continuous support, dedication, and guidance have been instrumental in helping me overcome obstacles and improve the quality of my work. I am sincerely appreciative of their tremendous efforts and unwavering belief in this project.I would also like to express my heartfelt appreciation to Mr. Ahmed, my project's external advisor from Ahmed Corporation. His invaluable advice, insightful critique, and vast wisdom have played a pivotal role in refining my thoughts and enhancing the overall quality of this book. I am truly grateful for his guidance and expertise.Furthermore, I would like to acknowledge Ms. Sultana and every individual who has contributed to obtaining the necessary resources and making this initiative possible. Your assistance, whether it was in sourcing information, conducting research, or providing logistical support, is deeply appreciated. This book would not have come to fruition without your invaluable contributions.I cannot overlook the individual who initially sparked the flame of inspiration within me to embark on this book-writing endeavor.

Your unwavering belief in my abilities, continuous motivation, and unending support throughout this artistic process have been instrumental in my journey. I am forever indebted to you for being my constant source of inspiration.I want to express my deepest gratitude to every person who has contributed to this project, no matter how small their role may have been. Each and every one of you has played a part in making this book possible, and your contributions have not gone unnoticed. Your support, encouragement, and assistance have been instrumental in bringing this book to fruition.Finally, I would like to give special credit to Kai, B.EE, and Tyson, the pen names that have accompanied me on this writing adventure. Your creativity, distinct perspectives, and unique insights have added depth and character to this book. I am honored to have had the opportunity to collaborate with you.To all of you who have been a part of this remarkable journey, I extend my deepest gratitude. Your unwavering support, guidance, and friendship have been invaluable. Thank you for believing in me and for contributing to the realization of this non-fiction book.With

sincere appreciation,

Elio Endless

EDITOR NOTE

1. Publisher Notes: This edition is a product of inspiration from other works, with a portion of its content derived from public domain sources. Elioendless, the creator, editor, and publisher of the ebook edition, utilized manuscripts, select texts, and illustrative images from public domain archives. Members can acquire this ebook from our website for personal use. However, please note that any form of commercial storage, transmission, or reverse engineering of this file is strictly prohibited.

Table of Contents

Preface ....

Dedication ....

Copyright ....

Acknowledgement ....

Chapter One ....

Chapter Two ....

Chapter Three ....

Chapter Four ....

Chapter Five ....

Factors Affecting Work-Life Balance

CHAPTER 1

Factors Affecting Work-Life Balance

INTRODUCTION

Human resources play a vital role in a country attaining economic development. The economic development of a country involves proper utilisation of its physical resources by its labour force and other forms of manpower, for the proper utilisation of the production potential of the country. Human resources which are a part of the service sector is the most significant contributor to the Indian economy. Work and life are the most important domains for most adults. Irrespective of his or her profession, every human being has to attain work and life balance. Balancing of work and life is a big challenge for all employees. Work-life balance is necessary not only for the workforce but the organisation too. When the employees become able to balance their work and life, it reflects on their performance and effectiveness in both the domain (Work and Life).

A right balance between work and life play an important role in attaining personal and organisational goals. Work-life balance has significances for employee's attitudes towards their organisation and their lives. Over the last few decades, the impact of the dramatic change in the social, religious, political, and economic environment has led to a rapid expansion in the number of women entering the paid labour force in India as elsewhere. Increased women literacy rate in India, the demographic changes are seen in the forms of increasing number of women in the workforce. In the 21st century, large numbers of women are working in different fields. According to the latest censuses (2011), 25.6% of women in India are participating in workforces. The increasing number of nuclear as well as dual-earner families have put considerable pressure on both men and women to manage their work and family.

The police profession has a challenging or even outright hostile work environment for women and men officers. Work-life balance is an essential problem in police personals. The job of a Police is one of the occupations that have been identified as the high level of stress. The responsibilities of police personals are varied and differed and interrogation of crimes. They have to respond to unexpected situations that may arise when they are on duty. The boredom of monotonous responsibilities, exorbitant workload, exposure to adverse and extreme environmental conditions, lack of communications, lack of appreciation, unsatisfactory career prospects, poor pay and allowances, conflicts, working in night shift, unscheduled working time, complex role assigned to the law enforcers make the job and life of police officers extremely difficult to manage. Moreover, police personals have to maintain orders and consequent reporting to higher officials. The police officers also experience interpersonal relationship problems. This accentuates the necessity of analysing the perceptions of police personnel work-life balance.

HISTORICAL BACKGROUND / EVOLUTION OF THE CONCEPT OF WORK-LIFE BALANCE

The work-leisure dichotomy was invented in the mid-1800s, as a result of industrial capitalism. In anthropology, a definition of happiness is to have as little separation as possible "between your work and your play." The expression "Work-life balance" was first used in the United Kingdom in the late 1970s to describe the balance between an individual's work and personal life. In the United States, this phrase was first used in 1986 (en.wikipedia.org).

The history of work-life balance begins in the latter half of the 19th century when reformers successfully campaigned against long factory hours and were able to demonstrate that reductions in working hours had no impact upon levels of output. During the early part of the 20th century, the campaign to reduce working hours continued through a series of pioneering studies that demonstrated the relationship between time spent at work and the level of output was a complex one. These studies also took account of the importance of motivation and morale, fatigue, concentration, and attention to reveal that there were conditions under which a reduction in working time led to increased production, and there were optimum arrangements for the length of working time and intervals for rest pauses, in particular circumstances.

During the **1960s and 1970s**, though the term work-life balance had yet to be coined, a number of factors can be identified that eventually gave rise to the current policy mix.

These included:

- health and safety at work;
- international competitiveness;
- equality; and
- the flexible labour market.

During the **1960s** the debate was very much about the extent to which paid overtime was "manufactured", as explained below. The analysis focused on informal workgroup organisation and the joint regulation of working practices, within a framework of collective bargaining. The approach was at the heart of the report of the Royal Commission on Trades Unions and Employers Associations in the late 1960s. The analysis built on the productivity bargaining experiences of the previous decade. Productivity bargaining recognised that groups of manual workers often exercised unilateral informal control over many aspects of their working practices. Case after case revealed that the control included the regulation of working hours where overtime was paid at premium rates. Long overtime hours were often not necessary but "manufactured" to boost earnings. The consequence was a low productivity culture, associated with low hourly rates of pay and long hours of work. The answer was to negotiate new productivity packages, which included significant changes in work organisation and working practices – including flexible patterns of work organisation increasing basic rates of pay and curtailing overtime working.

The **1970s** proved to be a turning point brought about by a wide range of factors, such as increased international competition, changes in technology, new forms of organisation, increased female participation, as well as changing and more diverse working-time needs of individuals. It was during the 1970s that regulation also began to recognise the importance of equality with the introduction of the Equal Pay Act in 1970 and the Sex Discrimination Act in 1975. Since then issues relating to social equity and justice have multiplied and become more prominent and explicit. It is argued that long working hours among men in the child-rearing years have disadvantaged women in two ways: they have made it less possible for men to share in childcare and home building, leaving the onus upon women to carry those responsibilities; they have made it less possible for women to compete for more senior jobs if a major criterion for promotion is commitment to the job, as demonstrated by long hours at work.

During the **1980s** the political focus was very much upon liberalising the economy, including the labour market. At the heart of labour market reform was the introduction of more flexible patterns of work – frequently referred to as "atypical forms of employment" (increased temporary/fixed-term employment and so on.). This took place at a time of a significant structural shift in the labour market with employment moving from the production to the service sector, which tended to favour female employment at the time. The introduction of more flexible forms of work was an essential stand in improving labour supply because it potentially allowed groups of individuals otherwise unable to enter the labour market the opportunity to do so. It was only during the **1990s**, especially the latter half of the decade that Government began to play a more interventionist role to give employees (and potential employees) certain rights concerning establishing a work-life balance that suited them. Most people think of only one notion relating to work and life: the work-life balance notion. Here is a picture of this evolution.

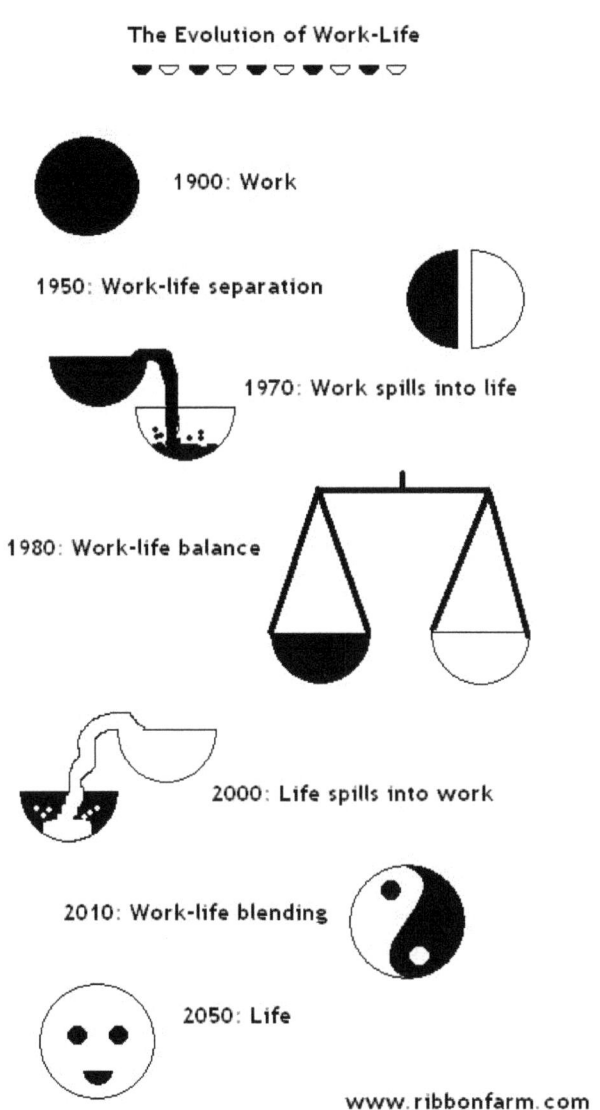

The Evolution of Work-Life

1900: Work

1950: Work-life separation

1970: Work spills into life

1980: Work-life balance

2000: Life spills into work

2010: Work-life blending

2050: Life

www.ribbonfarm.com

Figure 1.1: The Evolution of work life

Women's Values and Work-Life Balance

Work-life balance does not mean an equal balance. It means that the capacity to schedule the hours of professional and personal life to lead a healthy and peaceful life. It emphasis the values, attitude and beliefs of women regarding their age to work in organisation and balancing their work and personal life. When women achieved a successful work-life balance, she has job satisfaction and becomes highly committed and productive which succeeds in her career. However, in certain cases, the women are not able to succeed due to incapacity in balancing her work and personal life. She is unable to set her priorities. As result, she had withdrawn from her work due to simple reasons such as taking care of her children, aged in-laws, parents and other family pressure. If at the man is able to share some of her responsibilities, she would became a successful women.

Interplay of Multiple Roles

The literature does not contain one clear definition or measure of work-life balance. The six conceptualisation of work-life balance as (1) multiple roles; (2) equity across multiple roles; (3) satisfaction between multiple roles; (4) fulfilment of role (5) perceived control between multiple roles (6) relationship between conflict and facilitation; and

1. Work-life balance defined as multiple roles, "'Work-family balance reflects an individual's orientation across different life roles, an inter-role phenomenon" (Greenhaus et al., 2003).

2. Work-life balance defined as equity across multiple roles, Greenhaus and colleagues also explored the multiple roles definition of work-life balance further with a focus on equality of time or satisfaction across an individual's multiple life roles. The work-family balance was therefore defined as: 'the extent to which an individual is engaged in – an equally satisfied with – his or her work role and family role ... We propose three components of work-family–balance: time balance, involvement balance, and satisfaction balance' (Greenhauss and Shaw, 2003).

3. Work-life balance defined as satisfaction between multiple roles, Kirchmeyer (2000) defined work-life balance as: 'achieving satisfying experiences in all life domains and to do so requires personal resources such as energy, time, and commitment to be well distributed across domains' (Kirchmeyer, 2000). Clark (2000) also focused on personal satisfaction within the description of 'work/family border theory' and defined work-life balance as: 'satisfaction and good functioning at work and home with a minimum of role conflict' (Clark, 2000).

4. Work-life balance defines as a fulfilment of role salience between multiple roles, defined work-life balance as 'the extent to which an individual's effectiveness and satisfaction in work and family roles are compatible with the individuals' life role priorities at a given point in time.'

5. Work-life balance defined as a relationship between conflict and facilitation, work-life balance has been defined as an absence of conflict and a presence of facilitation: 'low levels of inter-role conflict and high levels of inter-role facilitation represent work-family balance' (Frone, 2003). This definition can also be tested through the assessment of the four bi-directional conflict and facilitation constructs: 'Balance is a combined measure whereby work-family conflict was subtracted from work-family facilitation, and family-work conflict was subtracted from family-work facilitation' (Grzywacz and Bass 2003).

6. Work-life balance defined as a perceived control between multiple roles, 'Work-life balance is about people having a measure of control over when, where and how they work' (Fleetwood, 2007).

THEORIES RELATING TO WORK-LIFE BALANCE

Several theories are explaining the relationship between work and life. The following are the leading theories of work-life balance:

1. **Conflict Theory**: This theory suggests that with high levels of demand in all the spheres of life, some difficult choices have to be made, resulting in some conflicts and possibly some significant overload on an individual occur.

2. **Enrichment Theory**: This theory postulates that the activities in one domain can enrich the experience in the other field instead of draining energy from the other domain. There are different terms associated with the enrichment such as facilitation (synergy), enhancement and positive spillover (experience). The work-family enrichment helps to improve the quality of work and life directly and indirect ways.

3. **Spillover and Cross over Theory**: In the context of work-life balance, spillover refers to positive or negative effects of an individual's working life on their personal life or family life and vice versa. This theory hypothesises that one world can influence the other in either a positive or negative way. There is, of course, ample research to support this but as a proposition, it is specified in such a general way as to have little value. We, therefore, need more specific propositions about the nature, causes and consequences of spill over. Crossover theory describes that the positive and negative emotions in one world immediately transferred to another world in closely connected individuals in work and family.

4. **Compensation Theory**: Compensation theory proposes that what may be lacking in one sphere, regarding demands or satisfaction, can be made up in the other. For example, work may be routine and undemanding, but this is compensated for by a significant role in local community activities outside work.

5. **Boundary and Border Theory**: This theory explained that the individuals create and maintain boundaries for work and non-work. Border theory is a refined version of boundary theory in which work activities and personal activities are differentiated

6. **Separate Sphere Theory**: this theory asserts that work, family as unique systems wherein the family is a domestic area for women, and work is a public area for men. This theory considers the sexual division of labour for the stability of society and to avoid conflict.

7. **Interactive Theory**: Interactive theory proposes the mutual interdependence between work and family. The joint and reciprocal influences of work and family

affect the social and psychological conditions of individuals either directly or indirectly.

8. **Conservation of Resources Theory**: Conservation of resources model offers a robust framework for individual's attempts to utilise and keep resources. Resources refer to the means of achieving objects, conditions or energies and personal characteristics that are valued by the individuals.

9. **Congruence, Integration and Ecology Theories**: Congruence theory showed that apart from work and family there is some critical variable influenced the work and life such as personality traits, genetics, education, and intelligence and socio-cultural forces. Integration theory is based on the holistic model of work-life balance. This theory emphasises that all the stakeholders (employers, workers and communities) shared responsibilities to rebuild traditional work life paradigms and better work-life balance. Ecology system theory refers to work and life are indicative, the experience and activities in both domains provide a practical effect. Later the ecology theory was converted into Person-in-environment theory.

10. **Work Life Management Theory**: Based on the self-determination theory, the work-life management model focuses on managing life through an autonomous self proactively.

11. **Gender Inequality Theory**: Gender inequality theory provides a unique perspective and gives insight into the unequal participation of women in labour market as compared to men

12. **Expansionist theory**: According to this theory the multiple roles are beneficial to both and women.

BENEFITS OF THE WORK-LIFE BALANCE

Work-Life Balance not only affects the individual but also affects the organisation. Therefore, today solving work-life conflict is the concern for all growing organisations and can be taken as a part of organisation development.

Benefits to the Organization

- Increase in individual productivity, accountability, and commitment.
- Better teamwork and communication
- Improved employee morale and commitment.
- Less negative organisational stress.
- Improved reputation
- Potential for improved occupational health and safety
- Good corporate citizenship and an enhanced corporate image

Benefits to the Individual

- More value and balance in daily life
- Increased Productivity
- Improved relations both on and off the job
- Reduced stress
- Able to meet work/personal/society commitments
- More time to do other things
- Increased ability to remain competitive in career advancement
- Benefits to the Society
- Reduce health care costs
- Encourage and enable family involvement
- Encourage/ facilitate volunteerism
- Happier people
- Reduce conflict/violence
- Better economy

Some more positive implications of Work-Life Balance are

1. Reduced absenteeism

2. Reduced Turnover

3. Reduced overtime cost

4. Client retention

5. Satisfaction among the employees (both monetary and non-monetary)

This would, in turn, help the organisation as well as individuals to grow and fulfil their needs. This would benefit in improving work culture and creating conducive work environment.

Post-Independence Challenges in Policing

History of modern Indian police can be traced back to 1861 when the Indian police act was passed. Necessary powers and functions are mentioned in this Act, and it is enacted during the British regime. The intentions of the British were quite clear. To them, police were to be an instrument of control of a colony, rather than a means to secure the people at large. In this scheme of thing, therefore, courtesy, ethical behaviour and decency had not much of a place.

The British legacy, unfortunately, got too much entrenched in the Indian police system. Even in the post-independence period, the police have not been able to shed the image of an agency of repression, misbehaviour, and harassment to the people

The Numbers and Representation of Women in Policing

Kerala was the first Indian state to have women in the police force, beginning with the first woman inducted into the then Travancore Royal Police in 1933. After that recruitment of women into the police in other states started only after independence, and even then it was sporadic at best. It was not until 1972 that the first woman was appointed to the Indian Police Service. By the time the National Police Commission completed its eight reports in 1981, women had accounted for a mere 3000 or 0.4% of the total police in the country. The brutal gang-rape and murder of young women in Delhi in 2012 call for more women in policing. At present 1,22,915 female police

1.1.2016, making up a national average of 11 per cent of the police. As per the rank, wise ASI& above comprise of 12,464, and H.C. & Constable is 27,304 (1:2.2). Coming to Kerala the total police population is 53,881 and in which women police consists of 2924 or 5.43 per cent as on 01.01.2016 BPRD

Jurisdiction of Kerala Police

Since the present study aims at investigating the work-life balance of women civil police officers in Kerala, it is necessary to be familiar with the structure, functions, and contemporary problems of the police organisation in Kerala. A brief description of the structure, conditions of service, features, and role of the police is given below.

Structure

The Police Act of 1861 made the establishment of organised police forces the responsibility of the various provincial governments then in existence in India. The constitution of independent India also placed public order and police including railway and village police in the State list. The organisation of police force in India is uniform throughout the States with minor differences in the structure and functions, which have been occasioned partly by recommendations of the state police commissions and partly as a consequence of the development of democratic institutions at the district level and below.

In the present system, the police in Kerala state is organised and maintained as one police force for the entire state under the command of a Director General of Police (State Police Chief). He is the representative of the state government for the administration of the police force throughout the state. He also advises on policy matters including internal economy, equipment, training and discipline of the force, its efficient organisation as a means of preventing and checking crime, preserving law and order and the efficient discharge of their duties by officers of all ranks. State Police Chief is assisted by Two Additional DGP's- South Zone and North Zone. Kerala Police is approximately 53,881 and in which women police consists of 2924 or 5.43% as on 01.01.2016. Kerala Police serve a population of over 35million residing in 14 revenue district, six municipal corporations, **87** municipalities and **941** grama panchayats over an area of 38,863 square kilometres with an average population density of 859 per square kilometre. Kerala Police Department investigates about 175,000 cases per year. The number of instances resisted in 2017 is 6.5 lakhs.

Governance of Kerala Police

The state head of Kerala Police Force is State Police Chief belongs to Director General of Police rank the officers of various ranks in ascending order, be as follows:-

- Director General of Police & State Police Chief.

- Director General of Police

- Additional Director General of Police

- Inspector General of Police

- Deputy Inspector General of Police

- Superintendent of Police

- Deputy Superintendent/Assistant Superintendent of Police

- Inspector of Police

- Sub-Inspector of Police

- Assistant Sub-Inspector of Police

- Senior Civil Police Officer/ Police Head Constable

- Civil Police Officer/Police Constable

For the proper administration, the Geographical area of the state is bifurcated as South Zone and North Zone, which is headed by Additional Director General of Police. Further, each zone is dived into two ranges viz Thiruvananthapuram Range and Ernakulam Range, Thrissur Range and Kannur Range respectively. There are five Police Commissionrates and 14 Police districts which are headed by District Police Chiefs, the rank of Deputy Inspector, General of Police / Superintendent of Police ranks. The Additional Director General of Police is in charge of a particular function such as Administration Headquarters, Modernization, PCR, CBCID, Intelligence, Traffic and Training.

Conditions of Service

A brief mention of the requirements of service in the police organisation would facilitate any attempt to unravel the pressures and strains that may emanate thereof.

a. Uniform: All police personnel except those serving in the Intelligence Departments have to wear a uniform.

b. Discipline: Regulations under Kerala Police Act and Kerala Service Rules Prescribe the procedure for disciplinary action, appeals, and revisions.

c. Hours of work: All police officers are liable to be called out for duty at any time of day or night.

DUTIES AND FUNCTIONS OF POLICE

General duties of police: - The Police, as a service functioning category among the people as part of the administrative system shall, subject to the Constitution of India and the laws enacted thereunder, strive in accordance with the law, to ensure that all persons enjoy the freedoms and rights available under the law by ensuring peace and order, integrity of the nation, security of the State and protection of human rights.

The functions of the police: - The Police Officers shall, subject to the provisions of this Act, perform the following tasks, namely:-

- To enforce the law impartially;

- To protect the life, liberty, property, human rights and dignity of all persons by the law;

- To protect the internal security of the nation and act vigilantly against extremist activities, communal violence, insurgency, and so on.

- To promote and protect arrangements ensuring public security and maintain public peace;

- To protect the public from danger and nuisance;

- To safeguard all public properties including roads, railways, bridges, vital installations and establishments;

- To prevent and reduce crimes exercising lawful powers to the maximum extent;

- To take action to bring the offenders to the due process of law by lawfully investigating crimes;

- To control and regulate traffic at all public places where there is a movement of people and goods;

- To strive to prevent and resolve disputes and conflicts which may result in crimes;

- To provide all reasonable help to persons affected by the natural or manmade disaster, calamity or accident;

- To collect, examine and, if necessary, to disseminate information in support of all activities of the police and the maintenance of security of the State;

- To ensure the protection and security of all persons in custody by law;

- To obey and execute all lawful commands of competent authorities and official superiors lawfully;

- To uphold and maintain the standards of internal discipline;

- To instil a sense of security among people in general;

- To take charge of and ensure the safety of persons, especially women and children found helpless and without support in any public place or street;

- To discharge any duties imposed by any law for the time being in force;

- To discharge such other functions as may be lawfully assigned to them by the Government, from time to time.

Thus, the police perform a vital role in acting as controlling radar, calculated to keep a society within its structural, cultural, and legal confines.

Importance of Work-Life Balance

Work-life balance is increasingly attracting attention at both the national and international levels. Organizations, which are unable to provide facilities to their employees in respect of managing, the balance of work and life must be ready for some adverse consequences regarding increased numbers of dissatisfied and unproductive employees. This ultimately leads to high labour turnover. Thus, it becomes imperative for organisations to have awareness regarding the overall aspects of Work-Life Balance. In the current scenario, Work Life Balance is considered as an issue of strategic importance to organisations as well as for the employees. There is a number of reasons for its growing importance. Due to the demographical and social changes, more women are entering the workforce. Women employees have become an integral part of the professional world. Still, the primary responsibility of women is considered as taking care of her family along with their professional role. Sometimes it creates a situation of conflict between work and life and in turn becomes a reason for the imbalance between work and family life.

Today women are working in almost all types of professions demonstrating that there is no gender difference at work. In many organisations, women are playing a vital role in uplifting the organisation. This is a positive development that women are making their presence felt in all occupations. On the other hand, for every woman, there is one more background to manage, which is home and personal life. Due to the increased demands at the workplace, the interface between work life and personal life assumes significance, and it demands more attention.

The Indian Police Department is unique in many ways; such as police personnel face high political interference in their day-to-day functioning, they face very high job demands, they work in unhygienic conditions, receive very little support from higher authorities, have to work in night shifts, have unscheduled working time. Considering these conditions of the demanding work environment and increase in crime rates, in particular women, the role of Women Police is highly required.

As a result, this study took into account of above-mentioned issues in work and how it has been impacting the Women Police Officers both in work and personal life. The results of this research would sheds lights on Women Police Officers Work-Life Balance and pave the ways for enhancing their undeniable role in improving in all possible way.

Research Focus: Women Civil Police Officers

The scope of the study is limited to selected factors influencing the work-life balance of women civil police officers such as what factors motivate them to choose a police career, their work-life balance, work-based social support, family-based social support, the perception of the job, job commitment and job and overall satisfaction. The geographical area of the study is confined to the state of Kerala. Women civil police officers are considered for the detailed analysis of the study. None of the studies has been done particularly aimed at the work-life balance of women civil police officers in Kerala.

Thus there is much scope for this research; the study findings will help to identify the factors motivating women civil police officers to choose their career in the police, the relationship between work-life balance, family support, workplace support, job commitment, job satisfaction and life satisfaction. Thus the study would help to the police department (a) To identify the motivational factors to choose the police profession (b) To know the support system available in the family and workplace,(c) To know their affective commitment, job satisfaction and life satisfaction.

Hence, the Government would be able to formulate policies for the recruitment, development, and deployment of Police professionals, thus leading to better talent force. Further, this study can help the society to understand the work-life of the women police officers.

Research Problem Investigation

The work-family balance has increasingly become a topic of interest in the field of research about the greater participation of women in the labour market, increasing a number of dual-earner families as well as significant and drastic changes occurring in the workplace. The woman's role in the family has always been emphasised by social pressures, consolidated in common cultural practices, by which men tend to offer support regarding being side-by-side rather than actuallly sharing of housework. Thus, women continue to carry the major burden of family and caring responsibilities even though their participation in the workforce is widely accepted.

The brutal gang rape and murder of a young woman in Delhi in 2012 called for more women in policing. At present there are 1,22,915 female police officers in India as on 1.1.2016, making up a national average of 11% of the police. As per the rank, wise ASI & above comprise of 12,464, and H.C. & Constable is 27,304 (1:2.2). Coming to Kerala, the total police population is 53,881 and in which women police amount to 2924 (5,43% as on 01.01.2016 BPRD). There is an increase in the number of women in police. However, in certain states, women police officers are close to nil. In the context of an increasing graph of crime against women in the country where overall crime against them rose from 3,29,243 incidents in 2015 to 3,38,954 incidents in 2016 (Bureau of crime record). The situation is pathetic despite the Union Home Ministry sending advisories in 2009, 2012 and 2016 to all the state governments and union territories to increase the strength of women police personnel to 33 per cent; still, they constitute only 7.28 per cent. The gap between the existing and sanctioned number of strength in the police force creates severe challenges in the society and the professional and personal lives of police personnel.

In this background, it is highly relevant to investigate the following major research issues.

1. What are the critical factors that influence women civil police to choose their career in the police?

2. What is the level of work-life balance among women civil police officers?

3. To what extent they experience social support from their family and work?

4. What are the positive outcomes of work-life balance?

5. Whether women civil police officers experience life satisfaction?

OBJECTIVES OF THE STUDY

The primary objective of the present research work is to identify the work-life balance among women civil police officers in Kerala. In order to accomplish this primary objective, the following specific objectives have been set forth.

1. To assess the opinion on the women civil police officers on the construct that influence work-life balance, family support, the perception of the job, department

support, superior support, co-worker support, job commitment, job satisfaction and life satisfaction.

2. To study the interrelationship between work-life balance, family support, the perception of the job, department support, superior support, co-worker support, job commitment, job satisfaction and life satisfaction.

3. To identify the factors that attracted women civil police officers to choose their career in the police.

4. To establish the conceptual model between various antecedents of work-life balance and outcome among women civil police officers.

LIMITATIONS OF THE STUDY

1. The study is focused only on women civil police officers in Kerala.

2. Data that are used for the analysis are based on the information furnished by the respondents; the respondents may not be consistent in their answers. Therefore, no generalisation can be made.

3. The study is limited to only the areas of Motivation to join the profession, Parental and Household responsibility (Family Life/Family Demand), Work Life (Job Demand/Work Challenges/ Job Characteristics), Work Life Balance, Family Support Departmental Support, Superior Support, Co-worker Support, Job commitment, Job Satisfaction, Life Satisfaction.

CHAPTER SCHEME

The first chapter 'Introduction and 'Theoretical Frameworks' deals with the introduction, historical background, meaning, definition, theories, benefits, organisational profile, the significance of the study, the scope of the study, research problem, objectives and limitation of the research and chapter wise division of the study

Chapter two covers the review of the previous literature relating to Work Life Balance, Family Support, Departmental Support, Superior Support, Co-worker Support, Job commitment, Job Satisfaction, Life Satisfaction. This chapter identifies the research gap through these literature reviews.

The third chapter discusses the methodology adopted for the present research study. It describes the design, sample, tools used, procedure of data collection and statistical techniques used for data analysis.

This fourth chapter gives a detailed analysis of concepts used in this study.

The last chapter shows the findings, suggestions, and recommendations, the conclusion of the study and scope for further studies.

Introduction to Work-Life Balance Among Women Civil Police Officers

Introduction to Work-Life Balance Among Women Civil Police Officers

INTRODUCTION

The core of the current research work is an investigation on the work-life balance among women civil police officers in Kerala. The study covers the antecedents and outcome of work-life balance. The researcher has attempted to review the relevant studies related to the present research work conducted so far to identify the research gap.

From the literature review, it is found that there are separate studies on family support, work social support, job satisfaction, job commitment, and life satisfaction in various sectors. Some studies show the relationship between these constructs in multiple areas. Similarly, some studies are done in the area of work-life balance informal sectors, and a few studies are there regarding work-life balance in women police officers at national and international level.

For the presentation of past studies, the relevant studies are classified into the following five sections. They are

A. Studies on work-life balance at the international level

B. Studies on work-life balance at the national level

C. Studies on work-life balance in police at the international level

D. Studies on work-life balance in police at the national level

Brief reviews of the literature coming under the above-stated heads are presented in alphabetical order in the following pages.

Work's Contribution to Meaning in Life

Clark et al. (2017) focused on the research was to examine the relationship between different organisational supportive factors and work-family outcome as well as the gender difference. 229 working adults employed full-time in a variety of industries from Michigan was selected through simple random method. Result highlighted that informal support factors were generally more significant than formal organisational support factors such as flextime and telecommuting. Supervisor support gave positive impact to men and women. The supportive work-family supervisor was related to higher job satisfaction among men and less quit intention to women.

Ward and King (2017) focused on work and the Good Life: How Work Contributes to Meaning in Life. The article aimed to assess the work orientations and social demographic factors that influence the propensity to seek meaning through work. The study highlighted the predictors and functions of meaningfulness at work.

Yuh and Choi (2017) in their study revealed that teacher's job satisfaction highly depends on directors and colleague support and their reasonably support also predicted quality of life after controlling the for age and marital status.

Adame et al. (2016) they conducted a study on Work-life balance and firms: A matter of women. According to their research, neither the presence or the absence of women does not determine the level of implementation of WLB policies. Likewise, the absence of organisational commitment to WLB leads to the lack of WLB policies.

Canonico (2016) putting the work-life interface into a temporal context: An empirical study of work-life balance by life stage and the consequences of homeworking. Findings reveal that homeworking may cause tension in the cultural climate relationship and negatively affect organisational performance.

Cicek et al. (2016) studied on a new antecedent of career commitment: work to family positive enhancement. According to their research, identity dimension of career commitment was influenced by the affect dimension and capital dimension of enrichment and by the affective dimension of positive spill over. The variance in the dimension of planning and resilience can be explained by the change in the level of spillover with negative direction.

Martínez-Pérez (2016) aimed to analyse life satisfaction under different childcare arrangements. The result highlighted that lone parents across Europe report lower levels of life satisfaction than those living in traditional families, comparing traditional (the nuclear family) with new (lone parenthood) family types.

Martínez-Pérez (2016) investigated the impact of child care arrangements on the working pattern, on mother's and father's life satisfaction capering traditional with new family types. The study was based on the 2011 wave of the European Quality of Life Survey interviewing a sample of representative adult individuals in 34 European countries. The result highlighted that traditional nuclear family type was most predominant across Europe as lone parenthood was widespread across central, eastern, and above all Nordic countries. The life satisfaction of mothers and fathers highly dependents on family structure. The lone parents experienced a lower level of life satisfaction than traditional families. The extent of formal and informal child care arrangement highly depend on personal constraints and public policies.

Szender et al. (2016) studied on the evaluation of satisfaction with work-life balance among U.S. gynaecologic fellows: A cross sectionals study. The study highlighted that family factors do not appear to influence satisfaction with WLB. The result shows those weekly working hours was a stronger predictor of WLB satisfaction.

Hoffmann-Burdzinska and Rutkowska (2015) researched on work-life balance as a factor influencing well-being. The primary focus was to identify the common features for work-life balance and well-being. The significant findings were a work-life balance, and welfare is firmly connected and has many common areas. They also highlighted the different scope of work-life balance.

Kima and Windsor (2015) in their research article on resilience and work-life balance in first line nursing managers. This study aimed to explore how first-line nurse managers constructed the meaning of resilience and its relationship to work-life balance for nursing in Korea. Analysis revealed that perceived work-life balance and resistance to being shaped by dynamic, reflective processes.

Nireekshan (2015) studied the issues of work-life balance, occupational stress and personal life stress among employees in manufacturing and IT sector. The findings revealed that an inverse relationship between the occupation stress experienced by employees and their degree of work-life balance. Also, the employees of manufacturing sector experienced a higher level of work-life balance than IT sector.

Pookaiyaudom (2015) published research article with the primary objective was to Assessing different perceptions towards the importance of a work-life balance a comparable study between Thai and international programme students". The result of the survey arrived by in-depth Discussion ending with a conclusion encompassing all aspects noted and then looks further to the importance and future implications of this research which presents the extra-curricular activities that university conduct increases students' quality of life and WLB.

Rostami (2015) identified the motivational factors of higher educated Iranian immigrant women, their work-life integration in the United States. The findings centred on the participants' need to find a meaningful balance between work- and home life. The family was a priority of all of the respondents, an influence that mirrored Iranian society values. The women who chose to immigrate felt pressure to succeed in all of their endeavours.

Alexopoulos et al. (2014) in their article exploring stress levels, job satisfaction and quality of life in a sample of police officers in Greece, a cross-sectional study was conducted using questionnaire method. The findings of the study was a higher level of perceived stress was related to a lower likelihood of being satisfied with their job. The male and higher ranked officers show the lower job satisfaction, and women show lower QoL about psychological health. The magnitude of the association between job satisfaction and QoL depends on age, gender, and rank.

Au et al. (2014) focused on sustainable people management through work-life balance: A study of the Malaysian Chinese context. The major goal of this paper was to examine the harmful effects of negative externality at both national and firm level by identifying practices that affect Malaysian Chinese's well-being in the form of work-life imbalance. The findings highlight the contextual elements in the macro-environment, such as government legislation and policy, societal values, and practices and the firm environment owner and leadership values, superiors' attitude come together to shape the overall experience of work-life balance among Chinese Malaysians. The result of the study was an eye-opener for the organisation. The state of current work-life practices in Malaysia fall short in some ways, which ultimately leads to an unsustainable human resource position for Malaysian firms.

Haar et al. (2014) examined the outcomes of work-life balance on job satisfaction, life satisfaction, and mental health: a study across seven culture. The research was conducted in Malaysian, Chinese, New Zealand Maori, New Zealand European, French, and Italian. The result of the study demonstrated that WLB was positively related to job and life satisfaction and negatively related to anxiety and depression across the seven cultures. Also revealed that individualism, collectivism, and gender egalitarianism moderated these relationships.

Huber (2014) examined the professionalism and the work-life balance among surgeons. The result shows that the practice of surgery was inherently stressful, and surgeons were at high risk for burnout and other stress-related disorders, particularly younger surgeons. The paper also highlighted that the physician wellness should be an integral part of the institutional quality improvement program and surgeons should develop personal strategies to manage stress and maximise job engagement regarding energy, involvement, and efficiency.

Kahya and Kesen (2014) studied the effect of perceived organisational support on work to family conflict: a Turkish case. The primary objectives of the study were the role of perceived organisational support on work-family conflict. The research highlighted that perceived corporate support hurts work-family conflict.

Kim (2014) research based on analysis of the effect of work-life balance on affective commitment and in-role performance and to explore the mediating role of emotional commitment to link work-life balance and in-role performance. The study was conducted in the Korean business context. 293 samples were collected through questionnaire survey method. The results demonstrated that there was no direct effect of work-life balance on in-role performance. However, the increased work-life balance effect on the positive impact on affective commitment. Also, the increasing degree of work-life balance rises affective commitment, and that affective commitment has a positive influence on in-role performance.

Marini (2014) studied the relationship between job satisfaction and life satisfaction: Empirical Evidence from Logistics Practitioners in a South African Steel-Making Company. This study aimed to investigate the structural relationships between job satisfaction and life satisfaction. The study followed a quantitative survey approach in which a three-section questionnaire was administered to 192 purposively selected logistics practitioners in a South African steel-making company. Positive, significant relationships were found between life satisfaction and two factors, namely, skills utilisation and remuneration. Weak correlations were found between life satisfaction and three job satisfaction factors, namely, teamwork, workplace flexibility, and autonomy.

Mellner et al. (2014) aimed to investigate boundary management preferences, the perception of preferred boundaries, and work-life balance among employees at a Swedish telecom company. The data collected from 808 respondents through a web-based questionnaire. The result highlights that most of the respondents experienced high preference of segmentation and low boundary control. The male responded in segmentation group showed better work-life balance and boundary control than their counterparts. Among integrators, there were no gender differences in either boundary control or work-life balance. The individual capacity for self-regulation in work was vital for high boundary control among both groups.

Michel et al. (2014) aimed to provide an empirical examination of the relationships between leaders dispositional effect, leader work-family spill over, and leadership. The results indicate that dispositional effect was a strong predictor of both work-family spill over and leadership. Further, the relationship between negative/positive effect and leadership was partially mediated by work-family conflict/enrichment.

Ong and Jeyaraj (2014) in their research paper titled work–life interventions: differences between work-life balance and work-life harmony and its impact on creativity at work. The focus of the study was to analyse the differences between the constructs of WLB and WLH using a cognitive dissonance approach and assessed the impact of work-life interventions using a cognitive dissonance on individual creativity at work. The results showed that participants in the WLB condition elicit higher levels of cognitive dissonance compared with participants in the WLH condition. The finds highlighted that an inherent difference in the constructs of WLB and harmony and work–life interventions adopting a WLH approach would have a more positive impact on individuals' creativity at work compared with interventions targeted at achieving balance.

Paula et al. (2014) aimed to develop a new measure for evaluating work-life balance. A longitudinal study was conducted in purposefully selected four heterogeneous 6983 sample of industries, including public service, health, education, finance, manufacturing and non-governmental organisation in Australia and New Zealand. Result demonstrated that work demands were the significant antecedent of work-life balance, while job satisfaction, family satisfaction, psychological strain, and turnover intentions were each significant outcomes of work-life balance. A new measure of work-life balance demonstrates robust psychometric properties and predicts relevant criterion variables.

Rudolph et al. (2014) studied on perceived social support and work-family conflict a comparison of Hispanic immigrants and non-immigrants cross-cultural management. The result of the study revealed that perceived organisational social support was associated with reduced work-family conflict for immigrant but not for non-immigrant Hispanics, and perceived supervisor social support was associated with reduced work-family conflict for non-immigrant but not for immigrant Hispanics.

Shakir and Noorani (2014) in their research paper work-life balance: a practice or myth in Pakistan - a quantitative analysis of the factors affecting the work-life balance of employees of Pakistan international airline corporation. The research aim of the study was to investigate the factors influencing work-life balance and its positive impacts on the personal and professional efficiency of the employees. The result indicated that the employees experience the imbalance in their personal and professional life. The study found the main reason was job content and family circumstances

Bruton (2013) study seeks to establish the meaning of work-life balance and goes on to examine the effectiveness of the workforce reforms in achieving their goal to support teachers in producing such a balance. The result shows personal capacity and personal control were pivotal in enabling staff in secondary schools to manage the work and non-work aspects of their lives to achieve an acceptable balance. Workforce reforms had not been effective in this respect. The differing perspectives of teachers and leaders in the schools were highlighted to identify the key factors, which affect the ability of an individual to achieve a work-life balance.

Carlson et al. (2013) aimed to evaluate the relationship between work-family balance and organisational citizenship behaviour via positive effect. The results of this study indicated that greater work-family balance was associated with higher supervisor reported OCB-Is and OCB-Os, and the positive effect mediated these associations.

Jacobsen et al. (2013) the primary goal of their article was based on a structured literature review of the three primary research perspectives welfare, working environment, and HRM. The result showed that a common interest in solving the problems of the overlapping working life, they do so with different methods and criteria for success, and offer different solutions. The study proposed the concept of overlapping working life to analyse how working life studies create meaning around quality issues of modern working life. Overlapping working, the focus was one of the multiple challenges faced by working people who are simultaneously individuals, citizens, and employees. The study proposes further research in initiatives aiming at improving the complementing and supplementing of the three perspectives especially about the facilitation of families with small children, an intensified focus on inclusive workplaces, and a higher degree of correlation between HRM, working environment, and welfare policies.

Komodromou (2013) this research examined the offering of work-life balance benefits, the value employees place on those benefits, the communication of the benefits by the organisation to employees, and their effect on employee attitudes and behaviours. The goal was to identify the impact on desirable outcomes when work-life balance benefits are offered to determine the usefulness to the organisation of providing such benefits. The results of the quantitative analysis showed support for a relationship between the offering of work-life balance benefits and perceived organisational support, perceived distributive justice, job satisfaction and OCBO.

Koubova and Buchko (2013) the purpose of this paper was to develop a conceptual linkage between life-work balance and emotional intelligence. Based on a review of the literature, it was suggested that life experiences contribute to the development of EI, which then moderates the individual's life-work balance. The effect of emotions on an individual's life environment was of primary importance in the development of EI, which influences the work environment. The level of emotional intelligence changes the effects of work experience on one's personal life significantly. Findings revealed that the level of EI was viewed as central to developing an individual's life-work balance, and the primary effect of one's personal life suggests that it is more appropriate to view work as a component of overall life satisfaction; hence the use of the term "life-work balance".

Maqubela (2013) the study focused on an exploration of parenting, normative expectations, practices and work-life balance in post-apartheid South Africa, 1994 - 2008 The research shows that the support networks mobilized by women are influenced by socio-economic and geographical mobility associated with the rise of the new black middle-class families brought about by the political change from apartheid to democracy. The migration of families from working to middle-class areas demonstrates the fluidity of mothering and coping strategies; while fathers remain free from childcare and family responsibilities.

Michel and Clark (2013) this study examined the perception of individual differences work-family conflict and facilitation, as well as the moderating role of boundary preference for segmentation on these relationships. Result revealed that individual differences were consistently predictive of self-reported work-family conflict and facilitation.

Panisoara and Serban (2013) studied marital status and work-life balance. The main aim of the study was to assess the marital status impact on work-life balance the findings show that the four categories of employees included in the research (unmarried, married without children, married with children under 18, married with children over 18) do not have a significantly different level of work-life balance. The finding of the research demonstrated that there was no significant difference in marital status and work-life balance.

Permarupan et al. (2013) propose to examine the organisational climate and employee's work passion and organisational commitment within academician of public and private Universities in Malaysia. The result showed that there was a causal link of right organisational climate, employees work passion and commitment in an organisation.

Umene-Nakano et al. (2013) the objectives of this study were to determine the relationship between work environment, work-life balance, and burnout among psychiatrists working in medical schools in Japan. They used a standardised scale to collect data from 704 respondents. Data collecting tool was questionnaire method. According to their result, the psychiatrists experienced a high level of emotional exhaustion, a high level of depersonalisation and a low level of personal accomplishment they also experienced the poor work-life balance and work experience satisfaction which led to burnout, and social support was helped to reduce burnout.

Brown et al. (2012) in their research, studied the poor summary measure of job quality. The survey data on job satisfaction and subjective well-being at work were informative. The result made a sensible conclusion about the meaning behind job satisfaction and information. The result of the study also understood the main reason for reporting workers satisfaction and dissatisfaction with their jobs due to their sociology.

Chen and Powell (2012) the purpose of this study was to suggest a reconciliation of the two research streams by proposing and testing a resource-based model of work-to-family enrichment and conflict. The result offers that an individual's work role engagement has two independent outcomes, work role resource gain and loss, and they separately mediate the relationships between work role engagement and work-to-family enrichment and conflict.

Clouston (2012) studied the influence of organizational workplace cultures on employee work-life balance. It explores the influence of organisational workplace cultures on the lived experience of work-life balance for individual employees. Findings identified that the social services setting provided greater temporal flexibility and supportive culture for work-life balance than healthcare, but that both organisations utilised cultures of power and performance to achieve organisational outcomes, irrespective of the impacts on personal or family well-being.

Ervin (2012) has done a Comparative Analysis of Work-Life Balance in Intercollegiate Athletic Graduate Assistants and Supervisors. The purpose of this exploratory study was to assess work-life balance in graduate assistants (GAs) and their supervisors by comparing their levels of work-family conflict, work-extracurricular conflict, job satisfaction, and life satisfaction. Secondly, the study introduced the work-extracurricular conflict construct. The investigation revealed significant differences between GAs' and supervisors' job satisfaction while determining they did not differ on work-family conflict, work-extracurricular conflict and life satisfaction levels.

Fatima and Sahibzada (2012) the purpose of the study was to identify causes of work and family role strain among university teachers of public and private sector institutions in Pakistan. Convenience sampling method has been used to get the responses from both public and private sector universities. A total of 84 responses from public sector universities and 62 responses from the private sector universities were included in the research. The study revealed a result that spousal supportiveness at home and colleague supportiveness at work contribute positively to work-life balance, whereas childcare problems, elder dependency at home and negative criticism at workplace contributed negatively towards work-life balance. This study concluded that concerning partner support male teachers are more satisfied with work-life balance as compared to females. The childcare responsibilities created a work-family strain among university teachers, and it was further noticed that elder dependency was doubling the burden of women than men. Work-life balance concerning colleague support provides evidence that female university teachers are less satisfied with their colleague supports as compared to their male counterparts.

Froese and Xiao (2012) studied the relationships between work values, job satisfaction, and organisational commitment of white-collar workers working in the foreign-invested companies in China. The result demonstrated that various facets of job satisfaction dependents the relationships between work values and organisational commitment. Employees' individualism and their willingness to take risks were related to multiple aspects of job satisfaction.

Idrovo et al. (2012) studied comparing work-life balance in Spanish and Latin-American countries. This paper aims to determine the level of awareness and implementation of family-responsible parameters like policies, enablers, practices, and culture, in Spanish and Latin-American companies, and their impact on work-life balance. The result revealed that Latin-American countries got a slightly higher number of companies that were supportive of work-family balance environment than Spain, but with lesser formal policies implemented and a stronger presence of enablers and practices. About the Policies in the companies was essential but might not be as effective if not accompanied

Jeremy (2012) this research addressed the gap in knowledge in understanding the extent to which job satisfaction is related to effective, continuance, and normative commitment. The purpose of this research was to provide an analysis of the extent to which job satisfaction is related to effective, continuance, and normative commitment. Using effective, continuance, and normative commitment main effects to predict job satisfaction results in an improvement in using organisational commitment to predict job satisfaction.

Khallash and Kruse (2012) studied the future of work and work-life balance 2025. This paper explores the concept of the future of work and identifies some of the challenges that Europe will increasingly face about economic, social, and demographic changes. The result demonstrated that the factors of work-life balance at present and alternative fictionalised situation for future work interplay between macroeconomic and the work-life balance.

Ma and Yin (2012) Did a study on the effect of work/life commitment to the work-life conflict. This study examined the relationship between work and life orientation and work interference with personal life or personal life interference with work of employees in China. Cluster analysis results showed that there are four profiles of direction: work orientation, life orientation, integration, and disengagement orientation. There are significant differences in work interference in personal life and personal life interference work between different profiles.

Michel and Michel (2012) this paper assessed the relationship between work-family enrichment and job satisfaction, as well as the moderating effect of human resource flexibility among faculty members. Results show that work-family enrichment positively leads to job satisfaction, while family work enrichment did not. Human resource flexibility moderates the relationship between work-family enrichment and job satisfaction. Human Resource flexibility was also relevant to the impact of family-work enrichment on faculty satisfaction.

Moon and Jonson (2012) this study examined the role of various strains on officers' organisational commitment to their agencies. The research highlighted that officer being less committed to their police agencies. Consequently, policies that attempt to alleviate those strains or stressors commonly faced by officers can increase the dedication and possibly the job performance of America's law enforcement officials.

Nip et al. (2012) in their research focused on a systematic review of the association between employee work time control and work-non-work balance, health and well-being, and job-related outcome. This review has shown that there are theoretical and empirical reasons to view WTC as a promising tool for the maintenance of employees' work-non-work balance, health and well-being, and job-related outcomes. At the same time, however, the current state of evidence allows only very limited causal inferences to be made regarding the impact of enhanced WTC.

Qu and Zhao (2012) researched on employees' work-family conflict moderating life and job satisfaction. The results implied that employees facing less conflict between work and family tend to carry positive aspects of daily life to the workplace. The results also support the value of managerial efforts to have an organisational climate that is welcoming to employees' families.

Rehman and Azam (2012) in their research article based to assess the different influencing factors on women's work and family roles in the unique Pakistani socio-economic and cultural environment. The purposive sample of 20 women entrepreneurs was selected who owned and managed their business for at least three years and had responsibilities towards family (especially married women). The findings of the interview data reveal that work-life balance has different meanings for different people. The majority of the respondents showed that childcare, time commitment was a key factor for imbalance. Spousal support was also considered necessary for a good work-life balance. Among other motivational factors, achieving work-life balance was also one most significant motivational driver for women entrepreneurs.

Wheatley (2012) the purpose of this paper was to reflect on the underlying conflicts associated with current work-life balance and travel-to-work policies, as employed in the organisation in the UK. A mixed method approach is used to ascertain whether professional work-group cultures limit the effectiveness of work-life balance policy and the extent to which spillover is present between work-life balance and transport preferences, especially in car use. The evidence presented in this paper suggested that work-group cultures prevent employees, especially women, from achieving work-life balance, there is spill-over between work and non-work activities, creating time allocation challenges, and stress, for dual-career households attempting to achieve desired work-life balance, and specific conflicts were reported in balancing work with travel-to-work, especially car parking.

Darcy et al. (2011) the primary research aim the paper was to explore the antecedents of work-life balance for employees as they progress through four identified career stages denoted by age (early career stage, developing careers stage, consolidating career stage, pre-retirement career stage). The research was cross-sectional and was carried out among a sample of 729 employees working in private sector (10) and public sector (5) in the Republic of Ireland. The findings revealed that work-life balance was a common problem among the respondent's life throughout all their career stages and not as significant in parents with young children.

Abendroth and Den (2011) in their research article based on support for the work-life balance in Europe, the impact of state, workplace and family support on work-life balance satisfaction. The present research paper was a study of the relevance of different types of support for work-life balance satisfaction and analysed the importance of state, instrumental, and emotional workplace and family support. The result showed that support for employee work-life balance satisfaction has a direct and moderating effect. Also confirmed that emotional support and instrumental support in the workplace have a complementary relationship. Moreover, emotional support from the family has a positive impact on work-life balance satisfaction than helpful family support

Chan and Qiu (2011) this study examines the relationship between loneliness, job satisfaction, and organisational commitment of migrant workers. This study found that migrant workers are satisfied with their jobs and are committed to their organisations and lonelier migrant workers have higher job satisfaction and the positive correlation with organisation commitment.

Currie and Eveline (2011) they conducted research on E-technology and work-life balance for academics with young children. The study revealed the use of metaphors such as invasion and intrusion of e-technologies into academics' homes. This help to establish boundaries to separate work and family life. The research highlighted that most of the respondents felt that having e-technologies at home. It was of more benefit to their work, but they came at a cost to their family life - delivering a blessing and a curse.

Kodagoda (2011) conducted qualitative research in professional and managerial women and their partners or family members. The focus of this research was to investigate how professional and administrative women combine motherhood with paid work in Sri Lanka. Their study was done on 23 mothers in administrative and professional positions working in a feminised sector, public health, and a traditionally male-dominated sector, public banking. Banking and health organisation showed both negative attention and low take-up rate on work-life balance practices; this research has confirmed that there was a different relationship between childcare and mothers employment, particularly for career advancement and in care gap. They showed low capacity in work-life balance.

Kossek (2011) the primary aim of their research was to develop an integrated model of workplace support on work-family conflict based on meta-analysis. This study used 115 samples from 85 studies comprising 72,507 employees. The construct used for the research was the relative influence of four types of workplace social support to work-family conflict. The variable considered were perceived supervisors family specific support, general support, organisational family specific and regulatory public support. Results showed work–family-specific constructs of supervisor support and organisation support were more helped to reduce work-family conflict than broad supervisor support and organisation support.

McMillan et al. (2011) the purpose of this article was to identify construct definitions and measurement tools for the work/life interface: conflict, enrichment, and balance. An understanding of these concepts was critical to HRD professionals because interventions designed to counterwork/life interface issues cannot be strategically created, and culture changes cannot be effectively addressed until the discipline understands the nature and the organisational implications of employees' work/life interface. A new construct called work/life harmony and the work/life harmony model is introduced to aid in the understanding of the work/life interface.

Miller (2011) the purpose of the dissertation was to examine how employees perceive their organisation's family-friendly policies as they relate to achieving a positive work-life balance. This study explores the impact on the eight New Belgium Brewing Company employees. The phenomenological research was used for the study. The findings revealed that employees were more committed, the culture was integral to the respondents' perception of the organisation. Relationships built in direct correlation to the organisational culture. Also revealing the participant responses were less about company policies and programs and more about participants working in a company that cared. Company size could be a factor in maintaining a sense of community.

Murphy (2011) in their research article aim was to identify the factors influencing work-life balance among senior managers in Call centre in Ireland. The study conducted in eight senior managers in Ireland and five senior members in Europe.The significant findings revealed that the economic slowdown was the underlying reason to implement work-life initiatives in the organisation. The personal situations directly affect the measures of work-life balance. The primary factors influencing in the work-life conflict were childcare responsibilities, long working hours, and job content. The modern technology has helped to some extent by allowing senior managers to be accessible instead of having to be present in the office.

Saif et al. (2011) examine the relationship between employee work satisfaction (job satisfaction) and prevalence of work-life balance (WLB) practices in Pakistan. The sample collected from 450 male and female layoff was working in two prominent organisations operating in Pakistan. The results depict that no significant differences were found in employee satisfaction and balancing their work life activities at all the stages of management (Top, Middle and First Level). While looking at the facilities the organisation (PTCL) was offering less work-life balance facilities and the employee in layoff survivors were unaware of the facilities available at the organisation for balancing their work and non-work activities.

Sarwar and Aftab (2011) aimed at quantifying the relationship between Work stress and family imbalance. The samples were collected from 500 working and married middle-level managers of the banks, having a child or children. The study demonstrated that there was a strong positive correlation between work stress and work stress family. The nature of job variable work stress and work stress individual was significantly equal, but the work stress family impact was not similar. However, in the case of other variables like job experience, type of conveyance, type of house and bank designation showed work stress and the family impact was significantly equal but work only stress impact was not similar. However, gender not significantly related to work stress and family imbalance. This showed that work stress and family stress lead to work-life imbalance

Tamini and Kord (2011) in their research based on burnout components as predictors of job &life satisfaction of university employees the results demonstrated a significant difference in scores of life satisfaction for males and females. Female employees showed significantly higher mean scores life satisfaction in comparison to male employees

Chiang et al. (2010) studied the moderating roles of job control and work-life balance practice on employee stress in the hotel and catering industry. The main aim was to study the relationship among job stressors, coping resources, and job stress. The results demonstrated that high job demands coupled with low job control and the availability of work-life balance practice resulted in higher level of stress.

Hunter et al. (2010) examined how employees benefit from team resources in the workplace, in both domains via work-family enrichment. The result demonstrated that individual with team resources was more likely to experience both works to family and family to work enrichment. Also revealed that enrichment mediated the relationship between team resources and satisfaction with the originating domain.

Kwan et al. (2010) in their research article focused on the impact of role modelling on protégés personal learning and work-life enrichment. The results of the study demonstrated that role modelling positively affects relational job learning and personal skill development. The individual skill development positively related to work-family enrichment.

Malik et al. (2010) studied the relationship of job satisfaction with the Work-Life Balance, turnover intentions, and burnout level of doctors. A sample of 175 MBBS qualified doctors across Pakistan. One of the key findings of this research was that work-life balance was a major contributor to job satisfaction and female doctors were more satisfied with their job compared to male doctors. The analysis provides evidence that the doctors who were better able to manage their work and life responsibilities have low burnout level, experience more job satisfaction, and ultimately result in less turnover.

Michel et al. (2010) research are based on Clarifying relationships among work and family social support, stressors, and work-family conflict. Results suggest that the antecedent model of social support provides the most appropriate homological network regarding the role that social support plays within this stressor–strain framework. Specifically, controlling for role involvement, work and family social support have the most significant effect on same-domain role stressors, which affect the cross-domain work-family conflict constructs. Primary theoretical contributions include a more clear and definitive understanding of social support's role in these stressor–strain relationships, the part of involvement within this homological network and the potential no symmetrical nature of the work and family domains.

Potgieter and Barnard (2010) conducted research based on the construction of work-life balance, the experience of Black employees in a call centre environment. The findings suggest that work-life balance was conceptualized as a continuous, subjective, and holistic valuation of satisfaction derived from multiple roles about the importance to the individual at a given point in time.

Weer et al. (2010) they conducted a study on a commitment to non-work roles and job performance: Enrichment and conflict perspectives. The result showed that the level and type of job occupied by the respondents have been responsible for the dominance of the adverse effect. The outside work dampens or promotes performance in the work domain.

Wickramasinghe (2010) research article Impact of time demands of work on job satisfaction and turnover intention he studied the software developers in offshore outsourced software development firms in Sri Lanka. The major findings of the study are job satisfaction partially mediates the relationship between time demands of work and turnover intention.

Willson (2010) this thesis aimed to examine the determinants and outcomes of mothers' work-life balance decisions throughout the early maternal years. Provide implications for the efficient use of labour, for gender equality in labour market opportunities and outcomes, and for motherhood wellbeing. The conclusions additionally provide insight into the extent that institutional factors constrain mothers' work-life balance decisions.

Zhang and Liu (2010) studied the antecedents of work-family conflict: review and prospect. The present study focused on identifying the influential factors of WFC from three levels that were individual, work, and family. The result highlighted demographic, and personality variables were affected on work variables like work stress, family-friendly programs and impacts of family variables like family demands and spousal interactions.

Beauregard and Henry (2009) in their research article focused on linking work-life balance practices and organisational performance. The research highlighted that the organisation need to modify the work-life method to increase corporate performance.

Bloom (2009) their research aim was to measure work-life balance and management practices in medium-sized manufacturing sectors in France, Germany, United States and the United Kingdom. Data collected from 732 firms included the mangers and non-mangers through the interview methods. Result demonstrated that work Life balance practice (child care, flexibility and subsidies) strongly influenced work life outcome(productivity). The management practices (better shop floor operation or stronger incentives) play only the weak impact on work-life issues. The firm has employees that are more skilled implemented more work-life balance practices. The U.S. multinational in Europe adopt more work-life balance practice than the management practices. The United States followed less free work-life balance practices than the European countries. France has more free WLB practices than the United Kingdom or Germany. The U.S. multinationals were located in Europe having significantly better management practices than equivalent in- U.S. multinationals and domestic firms. The management practices of the United Kingdom and France have significantly worse management practices than the United States and Germany. U.S. firms appear to be able to transport their better management practices to Europe. Do not transfer their worse WLB practices to Europe

Hara (2009) examined gender influence in their work, in their dealings with the public and career aspirations among female police in Ireland. The primary goal was challenges and difficulties experienced when combining work with their domestic caring responsibilities. Research established that female officers do not experience gender inequality while working in their units in their police stations on a daily basis or when in contact with the public, career advancement was extremely limited in part because of self-exclusion based on women's decisions about their caring responsibilities.

Lewis (2009) examined the nature and extent of support for dual-earner families in France, Norway, Britain, Portugal, and Finland. The data collected from 2363 full-time women employees from five countries through the survey methods. Result highlighted that gender role attitude, long hours of domestic work, long working hours, lack of state social support was the primary source for work-life conflict. The study revealed that Finland and Norway showed a lower level of work-life conflict when compared to France, Britain and Portugal due to their societal effect.

Lu and Siu (2009) conducted a study in work-family balance on Chinese employed parents, antecedents and outcomes of a fourfold taxonomy of work-family balance in Chinese employed parents. The result obtained from this study was that the childcare responsibilities, working hours, monthly salary, and family-friendly organisational policy were positively related to the conflict component of work-family balance. The paper also highlighted that new parental experience, spouse support, family-friendly supervisors and co-workers had positive effects on the facilitation component of work-family balance. In comparison with the inconsistent results of work-family conflict, work in family facilitation had consistently positive effects on work and life attitudes.

Michel and Clark (2009) demonstrated that work-family conflict and enrichment did not mediate affect-satisfaction relationships. The study also suggested a dispositional effect was a driving force behind perceptions of work and family conflict, advancement, and satisfaction.

Michel et al. (2009) focused on a comparative test of work-family conflict models and critical examination of work-family linkages. The study showed that direct effects drive work-family conflict models while indirect effects provide little incremental explanation in regards to satisfaction outcomes.

Morgab (2009) studied the impact of work-life balance and family-friendly human resource policies on employees' job satisfaction. This paper will look at the overall comfort of employees as it relates to work-life conflict. Family-friendly policies may help organisations to assist employees with balancing work and family. Conflict roles can spill over from the work domain to the family domain and from the family domain to the work domain. Time and technical connectivity are factors in work overload. Supporting employees could contribute to job satisfaction by offering alternative work schedules and family-friendly benefits. Organizations that offer flexible alternatives can engage employees and decrease job turnover.

Nadeem and Qaisar (2009) contributed towards a contemporary issue of human resource management that was work-life conflict in Pakistan. The study will analyse the factors related to work-life conflict and its impact on job satisfaction of employees at the three-management level of the organisation. The sample data comprised of 157 respondents belong to one private and one public service sector organisation in Pakistan. The study provides that job satisfaction was significantly negatively correlated with work to family interference and family to work interference. The policy alternative should be that supportive management was required to minimise the conflict between work and family. Top management should realise the importance of work-life balance and its adverse effect on job satisfaction.

Pichler (2009) examined work-related and household, family-related causes of WLB. Analyses have shown that household-related aspects, especially the presence of small children, contribute little to the explanation of WLB. To overcome the current shortcoming in measuring WLB in large-scale surveys, propose to concentrate on a more 'work-neutral' measurement of WLB. Instead of putting the cause of work-life imbalance already in the question-wording, one could formulate questions more neutrally.

Turner et al. (2009) conducted exploratory research on employees' perceptions of work-life in an Australian infrastructure construction project. The sample of 43 employees participated in semi-structured focus groups. The result of the study projected culture, project resourcing and the schedule demands of the construction stage of the project were identified as barriers for Work-Life Balance. The participant revealed that the project alliance delivery model, flexibility of working hours and the project management team's support for work-life balance would facilitate work-life balance in the project.

Willams (2008) examined work-life balance and role overload of shift workers in Canada. The survey was conducted among 19, 600 full-time shift workers between the age group of 19 to 64. The result showed that men and women working in shift felt the same level of work-life imbalance. However, in the case of work overload, the family type is an essential factor for women and industry for men. Certain elements were common for both men and women regardless of shift work and family type. The level of satisfaction with work-life balance and role overload were related not only to workers' schedules but also to a complex interaction of hours worked, self-perception and general feelings of well-being.

Wong and Ko (2009) studied the perception of work-life balance issues among hotel employees in China. 320 samples collected through snowball convince sampling method among full-time employees working in large and medium hotels at a different position in Hong Kong. The result highlighted that seven critical factors such as enough time off from work, workplace support on work-life balance, allegiance to work, flexibility on work schedule, life orientation, voluntary reduction of contracted hours to cater for personal need and keep the work and career the demands. Those factors were able to attain better work-life balance in the dynamic hotel environment

Lapierre et al. (2008) tested a theoretical model linking employees' perception of their work environment's family supportiveness to six different dimensions of work-family conflict and their job satisfaction, family satisfaction, and life satisfaction. The result highlighted that with a casual situation the employees working in an environment viewed as more family-supportive experience and lower level of WFC. The reduced WFC led to more job and family satisfaction, followed by greater overall life satisfaction.

Malik and Khalid (2008) aimed a qualitative analysis of work-to-life and life-to-work conflicts and work hour adjustments among bank employees in Pakistan. It indicated that the employees faced the work-life imbalance due to lack of social support and long working hours. The implication of the present study was the organisations capacity to recognise the heterogeneity and multiple obligations of the contemporary and diversified future workforce.

Michel and Hargis (2008) provide a higher degree of empirical clarity concerning the interplay of work and family by directly examining the indirect effect of work-family conflict linkages and the direct impact of segmentation linkages on work and family satisfaction outcomes.

Moylan (2008) did Information Communications Technology (ICT) enable achieving a better Work-Life Balance. (National College Ireland. ICT does help organisations and its employees respond to their clients in a fast, efficient and easy way regardless of whether they are still at work and their desk or if they are working from home or some other remote location.

Trefalt (2008) examined boundary work, the process through which individuals construct, negotiate, place, maintain and change the boundaries delineating their work and non-work lives. The result demonstrated that boundary work could not be fully understood by looking at organisational policies, work culture, and individual differences alone.

Grzywacz and Carlson (2007 focused on Conceptualizing Work-Family Balance: Implications for Practice and Research. The goal of this article was to develop a better conceptual understanding of work-family balance. The report defined work-life balance as the accomplishment of role-related expectations that are negotiated and shared between an individual and his or her role-related partners in the work and family domains.

Moore (2007) aimed to compare and contrast the experience of work-life balance and the impact of company policies. An Ethnographic study was conducted among the workers and managers of an Anglo-German automobile multinational company. The study partly used participant observation and interview method. The findings of the study revealed that the company's work-life balance initiatives mainly focus on the managers. Therefore, the managers display greater loyalty to the company. The workers were better able to achieve work-life balance. The result also showed that both groups demonstrated a more positive attitude to their work. The managers focused more on achieving status and the workers on personal satisfaction.

Schulz et al. (2005) discussed experiences over the last fifteen years related to work/life balance for a dual career engineering faculty couple. They revealed that dual career faculty couples face a unique set of challenges within the academic world. The first challenge was the original job search and finding two positions. The next problem to both was to make it through the tenure and promotion process. The third challenge is to have advancement opportunities. Along the way, the couple had to work together to develop a work-life balance plan to provide an environment for each person within the pair to thrive toward his/ her career goals and personal goals. Apart from their professional issues, they have to balance the day-to-day activities of a functioning household.

Byron (2005) did a meta-analytic review of work-family conflict and its antecedents. They studied to determine the relative effects of work, non-work, and demographic and individual factors on work interference with family and family interference with work. This study provides support for the bidirectional nature of work-family conflict and supports the notion that WIF and FIW have different antecedents, and the analysis suggests that demographic variables, such as sex and marital status, are alone poor predictors of work-family conflict.

Dex and Bond (2005) focused on measuring work-life balance and its covariates. This study was able to measure employees' work-life balance and found weekly hours of work was a critical determinant of employees' work-life balance, alongside their occupations, gender, age and caring responsibilities.

Peeters et al. (2005) study aimed to test a model that delineates how demands in both life domains are related to occupational burnout and distinguishing home and job demands. The result differentiates between work-home interference (WHI) and homework interference (HWI), and the mediating role of WHI and HWI was examined in the relationship between job and home demands on the one hand and burnout on the other.

Lavanchy et al. (2004) studied determinants of rural physicians' life and job Satisfaction. Identified and quantified factors that contribute to rural physicians' satisfaction with their jobs and life as a whole. The study revealed that most significant predictors of rural physicians overall life satisfaction were satisfaction with jobs, personal relationships, health, finances, and absence of depression.

Frye and Breaugh (2004) conducted a study to develop and test a model of antecedents and consequence of work-family conflict and family work conflict. The study revealed that use of family-friendly policies, hours worked per week, and supervisor support was predictive of work-family conflict. Also, as predicted, childcare responsibility and supervisor support were found to be related to family work conflict. Work-family conflict was found to be connected to both job and family satisfaction. Our research extends to previous research in some ways.

Scholaries and Marks (2004) aimed to investigate the impact of employer flexibility on work-life issues and negative spillover from work to non-work life on the attitude of software developers. Data collected from the 245 employees working in a two-software organisation in Scotland. The result showed that the fair treatment with work-life issue significantly effects on work-related attitude. The employees experienced the same degree of work-life imbalance. However, employees were in this industry relatively individualistic in orientation and highly marketable they show their attachment to their organisation and were highly dependent on the benefits they received from the organisation.

Perrons (2003) the study conducted on the new economy and the work-life balance: conceptual explorations and a case study of new media. The research methodology used in this study was 55 in-depth interviews with new media owners, managers and some employees in small and micro enterprises, evaluates their claim. The focused area of their research was gender-differentiated patterns of ownership and earnings; flexible working patterns, long hours and home working and considers whether these working patterns were compatible with a work-life balance. The findings showed that new media creates new opportunities for people to combine interesting paid work with caring responsibilities, a marked gender imbalance remains.

Allen (2001) focused on the global employee perceptions of work organisation family-supportive Policies. The results revealed that Family Supportive Organisational policies mediate the relationship between family-friendly benefits available in the organisation and its depends on work-family conflict, affective commitment, and job satisfaction. FSOP also negotiated the relationship between supervisor support and work-family conflict.

Clark (2001) examined the effect of workplace cultures such as flexibility of working hours, flexibility of the work itself, and supportive supervision on five aspects of work-family balance work satisfaction, home satisfaction, work functioning, family functioning, and role conflict. A cross-sectional study conducted in 179 sample from United State different families and workplace. The findings of the survey highlighted that flexibility of work helped to increase the work satisfaction and family well-being. The Flexibility of work times was not associated with any work or personal outcome. The supervisor's support helped employees to increase their organisational citizenships behaviour. The study also demonstrated that interactive effects between aspects of culture and individuals' characteristics showed that work-family balance was lower among employees with a large number of children and supportive supervision.

Hill et al. (2001) focused on the influence of job flexibility in the timing and location of work on work-family balance. Results indicate that perceived job flexibility was related to improved work-family balance after controlling for paid work hours, unpaid domestic labour hours, gender, marital status, and occupational level. The study also highlighted that same workload with job flexibility helped to balance work and life.

Saltzstein et al. (2001) did a study on family-friendly policies on attitudes of federal government employees. The paper examined the theoretical framework regarding the relationships between work and family demands, family-friendly policies, satisfaction with work-family balance, and job satisfaction for diverse groups of employees with different personal and family needs. The finding of the study revealed that different options in "family friendly policies" were used to different leave by disparate groups of federal employees. The research identified that use of family-friendly policies had very diverse effects on both employee satisfaction with work-family balance and job satisfaction, within and across various groups of similarly situated employees.

Sirgy et al. (2001) developed a new measure for quality of work life based on need satisfaction and spill over theories. The measure was designed to capture the extent to which the work environment, job requirements, supervisory behaviour, and ancillary programs in an organisation. The study was conducted among two university employees and the third one accounting firms. The results from the pooled sample provided support for homological validity to the new measure.

Edwards and Rothbard (2000) purposed to translate work-family linking mechanisms into causal relationships between work and family constructs. The result highlighted that work-family linkages might operate differently for different types of work and different family structures.

 Frone et al. (1997) developed and tested an integrative model of the work-family interface. The model provides a general framework to help organise past research and guide future research on the work-family interface.

Adams et al. (1996) aimed to draw upon both the work-family conflict and social support literature to further understanding of the joint influence of these factors on well-being. The participants in this study were 163 full-time workers living with at least a family member in Michigan. The study indicated that the relationship between the work and family effect on job and life satisfaction. The association was either positive or negative, those who received family emotional and instrumental support showed a lower level of family interfering with work simultaneously higher level of work interfering with a foretold family with lower levels of family emotional and helpful support.

Kopelman et al. (1983) in this paper a model of work, family, and inter-role conflict: a construct validation study examined the construct validity of three scales to measure work conflict, family conflict, and inter-role conflict. Acceptable reliabilities were found, correlational and path analytic evidence was supportive of predicted and non-predicted relationships.

STUDIES ON WORK LIFE BALANCE AT NATIONAL LEVEL

Suva and Subymon (2017) conducted a study on Factors Affecting Quality of Work Life: An Analysis on Employees of Self-Financing Colleges in Thiruvananthapuram District. The study has twofold objectives to test the factors influencing on quality of work life of the employees in the selected self-financing colleges in Thiruvananthapuram district and finally, to understand the impact of identified variables of QWL on job satisfaction. The outcome of the research indicates that six out of seven factors have a significant influence on the quality of work life and the remaining factor has no significant impacts on quality of work life.

Kumaraswamy and Ashwini (2016) the primary aim was to identify the impact of various factors affecting Work-life Balance of women employees working in Public and Private sector Bank. 150 samples selected from both banking sector in Mysore city. The results as indicated revealed that Work life-related factors have a significant impact on the Work/Life Balance of the public and private sector bank employees.

Sakshi et al. (2016) studied work-related variables and work-life balance: a study of nurses in government hospitals of Himachal Pradesh. The findings of the study demonstrated that there is a significant correlation between various work-related variables and work-life balance (and its dimensions). Work-related variables, viz., task variety, work ambiguity, work autonomy and work role overload have a significant impact on the work-life balance of the respondents.

Salim and Mallika (2016) conducted a Study on Institutional Factors Leading to Well-Being among Faculty Members of Self Financing Business Schools in Kerala. This study was focused on more than 600 academicians from different business schools to understand what factors leading to a state of well-being among faculty members of self-financing business schools in Kerala. The study included the micro and macro aspects of faculty well-being. Based on the research, he concluded that educational institutions generate intrinsic motivation and commitment among the faculty members to raise the perceptions of well-being among its faculty members and focused on a balance between organisational productivity and employee well-being for sustainability of the high-performance work systems.

Dolai (2015) did research to measure work-life balance among the employees of the insurance industry in India. The comparative analysis of the work-life balance scores of different demographic profiles could not suggest that there were statistically significant differences in the perception of work-life balance across these demographic groups.

George (2015) studied Job-related stress and job satisfaction: a comparative study among bank employees".Results indicated that employees from different sectors of the bank had a different level of job Satisfaction and job-related stress. Further, it was revealed that public sector banks have lower job-related stress when compared to private sector banks and new generation banks; and higher job satisfaction when compared to new generation banks.

Jawahar and Soundria (2015) studied the impact on work home support on individual and organisational outcomes. The study was carried out of 215 women employees, working in southern railway of Kerala and Tamilnadu. Correlation and multiple regression analyses were used to interpret the data. The results demonstrate that there is a positive relationship between SWH and factors that constitute IOOC.

Maharshi and Chaturvedi (2015) did research based on the factors affecting the work-life balance of women employees working in public and private sector banks of Rajasthan. The study was demonstrated the four key factors were influenced that work-life balance among women employees in the banking sector. These factors key factors were a personal commitment, job productivity & performance, work task and time management. The result of the analysis showed that personal responsibility was a most crucial factor for work-life balance of women employees.

Nireekshan (2015) studied the issues of work-life balance, occupational stress and personal life stress among employees in manufacturing and IT sector. The findings revealed that an inverse relationship between the occupation stress experienced by employees and their degree of work-life balance. Also, the employees of manufacturing sector experienced a higher level of work-life balance than IT sector

Ramesh and Sakthivel (2015) the purpose of the study was to identify the work-life conflict among employees working in Kerala Co-operative Milk Marketing Federation Ltd. The study showed the respondents faced the family conflict, work conflict, work interfering with family conflict and family interfering work conflict.

Satyanarayana and Shanker (2015) the study examined the work-life balance of employees in the IT Enables Services sector and attempted to identify the association of work-life balance with age, gender, marital and parental status, income and work experience of the respondents. The study indicates a significant association of age, parental status on 'work interference in personal life.

Manju and Goswami (2014) proposed empirically tested model on the relationship between two domains work and family and their influence on work to family interference and family to work interference. The model also tries to correlate various constructs of work-life conflict to the organisational outcomes and individual outcomes.

Rasheed and Wilson (2014) in their research paper, "Over Education and the Influence of Job attributes: A Study Conducted in the City of Kochi" show that even though explicitly the employees are being compensated by the external attributes of the job internally they are dissatisfied due to the low intrinsic satisfaction.

Walia (2014) researched work-life balance of bank employees: a comparison with Indian banks. The aim of this paper to compare the work-life balance of employees working with public and private sector banks. According to her research, there was a significant difference between the public and private bank employees on the dimension of work-life balance. However, found that no gender differences were found in the work-life balance or any of its dimension both the employees working in private and public bank.

Delina and Raya (2013) studied the factors affecting the work-life balance of married workers in Academic, Information Technology and Health Care sectors. A total of 180 sample collected from Pondicherry through questionnaire survey method. This study was able to measure the work-life balance of working women .Result revealed that married working women were experiencing difficulty in balancing their work and personal life irrespective of the sector they were into, the age group they belong to, the number of children they have and their spouse's profession. However, the IT sector working professionals were experiencing more difficulties in balancing work and family than academic sector working women, and the health sector working women respectively.

Kanthi (2013) the primary aim was to find out the perception, procedures and facilities of Work-life balance of employees in selected units at Hyderabad district, to examine the attitudes of respondents on specific areas of work-life balance in two Electrical companies. Due to some economic, family problems, inefficiency, lack of commitment some of the sample expressed their inability to balance their work. The work-related variables like long working hours, compulsory overtime, insisting more stress-related job activities, non- flexible and closing time and other factors partially influencing the employees in the form of absenteeism, labour turnover, frustration, low morale and motivation which leads to an imbalance of both work and life. BHEL employees were more satisfied with all the above practices than VE employees were.

Nair (2013) emphasises the work-life balance of employees of IT organisations in Technopark, Trivandrum. 305 executives from the IT organisation Technopark, Trivandrum were surveyed for the study. The sample was drawn from all the three levels of management using convenience sampling. The study reveals that some of the work demand has provided negative interferences in the family lives of employees and has wide differences across gender, nature of the job and the level of management. The study confirms that a proper work-life balance will provide job satisfaction of employees, which in turn will create organisational success and develop a competitive advantage for IT organisations. The company should focus on providing efficient Work-Life Balance policies and programs to ensure proper Work-Life Balance, which will help them to improve the employee productivity and to control the attrition rate. Above all the employees themselves should adopt certain precautionary methods for self-management, which should include a proper time utilisation reducing burnout and stress.

Pathak (2013) the primary objective was to investigate the overall quality of work life and job satisfaction of textile workers in Madhya Pradesh. The result revealed that perception about the quality of work life differs according to a different level of quality of work life and time shift and the understanding of job satisfaction and significantly higher in the high level of workers than the middle and lower level workers.

Sankar and Raj (2013) studied on balance of work and family life of women employees in sago industry in Salem district. The purpose of the study was to examine the factors contribute to work-life balance and its consequences. The paper identified the key factors lead to imbalance were the workload, job design, discrimination. Keeping good relation with male workers was the solution to reducing the imbalance of work and family life.

Dash et al. (2012) this study was conducted with the twin objectives of establishing the psychometric properties of the measuring work-life balance and examine the perception of work-life balance across IT Professionals based on different demographic parameters. The data was collected from a random sample of 224 IT professionals working in Bangalore. The scale used in this study was Hayma (2005). Result demonstrated that scale was a valid and reliable scale for measuring WLB. However, the comparative analysis of the work-life balance scores of different demographic profiles could not suggest that there was a statistical difference in the perception of work-life balance across these demographic groups.

Miryala and Chiluka (2012) examine the level of WLB among teachers of different educational institutions; analyses gender wise issues, the relationship between age and WLB and various elements of WLB practices adopted by

Santhi and Sundar (2012) in their paper entitled study on the work-life balance of women employees in information technology industry. The purpose of the study was to identify the significant factors contributing to work-life balance among women employees in I.T. industry. The present study revealed that various factors were contributed work-life balance different cadre and most of the respondents were satisfied with the current work-life initiatives.

Thriveni and Rama (2012) the primary objective of the study was to determine the significant relationship between demographic variables and work-life balance of women employees working in the different profession at Bangalore. The primary data collected from 240 women employees working in various occupations in Bangalore city. The study revealed that there was a significant relationship between a demographic variable and work-life balance of women employees. The relationship between demographic variables and work-life balance of employees an vital input in designing appropriate policies for employees to address work-life balance issues.

Viyayshri (2012) this study aims to explore the relationship between support and employee outcomes of work-life balance in the service sector with specific reference to Pune City. In the relationship were examined. Two hundred and sixty-three questionnaires were distributed to six different types of organisations falling under service sector viz Banking and Financial services, Hospitals, Hotels, IT & ITES and Education and other. The findings of this study suggested that three kinds of support (organisational support, family support, and self-support) were positively related to employees' work-life balance. However, no significant relationship was found between the availability and usage of the work-life balance policies and employees' work-life balance. The focus of discussions revealed that while each organisation had various formal and informal work-life balance policies available, there were a significant number of barriers prevalent in workplaces, which made it difficult for employees actually to use these policies.

Chawla and Sondhi (2011) examine the work-life balance among Indian Women. The study revealed that Indian professional was looking for supportive workplaces that help them manage their multiple roles. The positive, supportive workplace spillover effect on the commitment and low attrition rate and at the same time enhance an individual's Work-Life.

Valk and Srinivasan (2011) focused on work and family-related factors that influence the work-family balance of Indian women IT professionals. 113 women IT professionals in software sector were interviewed under a semi-structured interview protocol. The researchers used inductive analysis. The narratives reveal six significant themes: familial influences on life choice, multi-role responsibilities and attempts to negotiate them, self and professional identity, work-family challenges and coping strategies, organisational policies and practices and social support.

Baral and Bhargava (2010) investigated Work-family enrichment as a mediator between organisational interventions for work-life balance and job outcomes. Data were collected from 216 managerial employees through a structured questionnaire from four organisations in India representing manufacturing and information technology sectors. The analysis was done using multiple regressions. The result showed that Job characteristics were positively related to job satisfaction, effective job commitment, and organisational citizenship behaviour. The support from the immediate superior and work-family culture was positively related to job satisfaction and affective commitment. However, in the case of work-life benefits and policies found no significant association with any of the job outcome measures. Job characteristics and supervisor support were positively related to work-to-family enrichment. Work-to-family enrichment mediated the relationships between job characteristics and all job outcomes and between supervisor support and affective commitment.

Gani and Ara (2010) attempted to study the causes, consequences and correlated of work-family conflicts among dual-career women. The study has been carried out in Kashmir valley among 200 women working in different white-collar situations, belonging to various social, economic, cultural, demographic, and professional group categories. The primary data was collected using written questionnaires, direct oral interviews, and observations. The results of the study were analysed with the help of simple average scoring scales, chi-square tests and ranking methods. The results suggest that many factors contribute to making role conflict of working women a reality. The sources of conflict were dependent on the availability of various support system within and outside the family as well as the organisation where she works.

Rangreji (2010) focused on emotional intelligence about employees work-life balance in IT organisations. The sample consisted of 355 IT employees from Bangalore city. The significant findings of the study were the three significant behaviours of work that interferes with personal life were unhappiness with the amount of time for non – work activities followed by missing own activities due to work and putting personal life on hold because of work. It was found that IT employees were high on the regulation of emotion in the self, followed by appraisal and recognition of emotion in others, use of emotion to facilitate performance and assessment and expression of excitement in the self.

Sirajunisa and Panchanatham (2010) the objective was to find out the influence of occupational stress and work-life balance dimensions of women professionals. The result of the survey highlighted that Women employees are working worrying about personal problems in office space and thinking about profession related problems at home.

Kanwar et al. (2009) studied on work-life balance and burnout as predictors of job satisfaction in the IT and ITES industry. The present study examines the impact of work-life balance and burnout on job satisfaction in the context of the Information

Technology, and IT Enabled Services industries. The findings reveal that work-life balance and job satisfaction were positively related to each other, de-motivation, exhaustion, and meaninglessness were negatively associated with job satisfaction.

Sen (2008) studied the relationship between job satisfaction & job stress amongst teachers & managers. The result of the study demonstrated that teachers experience low job Satisfaction and they face Job Stress while in case of managers the two do not seem to associate.

Thomas (2007) aimed to examine the perceptions of women professionals in Kerala, regarding their family and professional roles, with an understanding of the issues that they regard as enabling or constraining them in achieving family and work-life balance. The sample size was 350, and it consisted of 100 Doctors 100 Engineers, 100 Lawyers, and 50 Chartered Accountants. Structured Interview Schedule was the tool used in the present study. The findings disclose that women professionals were highly motivated in their careers. The study also unveils the presence of glass ceiling that denies the women professionals their rightful place in the occupational hierarchy

Bryant and Constantine (2006) in their research article on multiple role balance, job satisfaction, and life satisfaction in women school counsellors, findings revealed that multiple role balance and job satisfaction were each positively predictive of overall life satisfaction, even after accounting for the effects of age, years of experience as a school counsellor, and location of school environment.

STUDIES ON WORK-LIFE BALANCE IN POLICE AT NATIONAL LEVEL

Nerurkar (2014) did a research-based Stress among Mumbai Police Personnel. The researcher has attempted to identify the reasons for such stress, coping strategies and compare the stress among Mumbai police force based on designation and gender. The study revealed that same level of stress was experienced based on gender and designation. Th main source of stress due to nature of their work, lack of sleep, lack of support from the superior, interference in family life and stagnant role.

Vilas et al. (2014) researched coping strategies used by police for managing stress. The result showed that to adjust role stress, male police in comparison to those of the female police use more of passive coping. Strategies like daydreams, complaining, smoking, taking alcohol, writing stress diary, sleeping more and quitting job. Female police have been found to rely more on physical exercise meditation, yoga and so on to relax and burn the extra energy induced by stress in comparison to the male police

Padma and Sudhir (2013) examined the role of family support in balancing personal and work life of women employees. The study conducted on Female Police Personnel, which was conducted in Andhra Pradesh State Police Department on Women Police. The sample consists of Constables and Head Constables. The results revealed that Women with the dependent elder care need to be given a helping hand to balance their personal and professional works.

Srinivasan and Ilango (2013) aimed to find out various factors of socio-economic condition having a positive impact on the development of family and society as well as the police department. A study was carried out in four women police station in Trichy district. The main finding of the study showed that women police was not recognized by the higher male officers even their performance was excellent. Majority of the respondents are not satisfied with their salary while comparing their working hours. Majority of the respondents are leaving their children with their parents due to lack of time to take care of their children. Even after marriage, one-third of the respondents are helping their parents economically.

Vijayalakshmi (2012) focused was on work-life balance satisfaction among women police personnel in Hyderabad. The present study explores aspects like to measure the level of satisfaction as perceived by the women respondent employees in the police determinant of work-life balance, to identify the significant factors that influence the work-life balance among various categories of women employees in the police department. The findings show that women in the police department are dissatisfied and have some incontinence in work-life balance.

Usha and Geetha (2010) studied the socio-economic profile of odd hour working people and to examine the problems women face in their work environment and at home. A sample of 500 respondents from the universe of which 150 nurses, 210 business transcriptionist and 140 police personnel from Coimbatore Corporation area. The main statistical tool used by this research was Kruskal Wallis chi-square test, Spearman's rank correlation, factor analysis. The findings of the study revealed that women were dissatisfied with the quality of work life and faced family-related issues and personal problems irrespective of their occupation.

STUDIES ON WORK LIFE BALANCE AMONG POLICE/LAW ENFORCEMENT AT INTERNATIONAL LEVEL

Duxbury and Higgins (2013) aimed to identify the cause and consequence of work overload on the work-family conflict in police sector. The sample selected for this was 4500 police officers working for 25 police forces across Canada. The result showed shift work, low levels of control at work, high levels of overload, work interferes with family leads lower levels of job satisfaction, commitment, stress, intents to turn over and depressed mood. Staff in understaffed police organisations was the reason for high levels of role overload. The study suggested that introduce supportive manager, perceived flexibility, control over work and control over the family.

Tim and Sinclair (2013) focused on to identify key aspects of the status of women police internationally. Limited data on rank and deployment indicated overall improvements. Available longer-term trend data suggested that growth in female officers was slowing or levelling out. The study showed that an urgent need to improve gender-based statistics maximising the participation of women in policing.

Sachau et al. (2012) researched Work-Life Conflict and Organizational Support in a Military Law Enforcement Agency. The objectives of the study were to find out the work-life conflict and organisational support for work-life balance their impact on job satisfaction and turnover intentions in military law enforcement personnel. The article gave the result that the Perceived social support, especially at the organisational level, was negatively correlated with work-to-family and family-to-work conflict.

Matsch et al. (2009) in their research on the perceptions of work-life balance between military law enforcement personnel and their spouses. The goal of their research was to analyse the level of military law enforcement agents; their spouses shared similar perceptions of work-life conflict, and organisational support. Based on their study revealed that Agents and spouses shared very similar views regarding the Agents' work-life conflict and corporate support. .Both the Agents and their spouses perceived greater support for work-life balance from immediate supervisors than from the organisation as a whole.

Brown (1998) examined factors lead to discriminatory treatment of women police officers serving in forces in England and Wales. Results indicated that women police experienced the widespread exposure to harassment and other forms of unfair treatment. The persistence of discrimination is demonstrated, and policemen's resistance to women colleagues is discussed regarding occupational culture.

Koenig (1978) aimed to study the public attitude towards women in law enforcement in U.S. Result showed the role of the woman in law enforcement had changed markedly in the last century, as have the similar attitudes of the public toward women in general. The role of the policewoman has gradually shifted from one of a caretaker for incarcerated women and comforter of lost children to that of a bona fide law enforcement official. Although proper dress and manner are no longer the crucial factors in the orientation manuals for policewomen, female officers are still overly represented in caretaking and clerical duties in many U.S. cities. Male officers have yet to accept females as their equals in all phases of law enforcement.

Ercikti et al. (2011) in their major study determinants of job satisfaction among Police Manager, examines the levels of job satisfaction among police managers. The findings indicate that police managers have higher levels of job satisfaction than the research on their line level counterparts reports. Years of service, feedback on the job, and involvement in COP and Compstat programs were significant predictors of job satisfaction among this sample of police managers. It appears that participation in COP and Compstat programs can enrich the jobs of police managers.

IDENTIFICATION OF RESEARCH GAP

From the previous literature on a related area, it is found that different studies have been carried out by several researchers and institutions in the area of work-life balance. However, no studies have been conducted on the work-life balance among women civil police officers in Kerala. Similarly, there had been no studies on the factors attracted to join the profession, work-life balance, family support, department support, co-worker support, superior support, the perception of the job, job commitment, job satisfaction and life satisfaction. In this scenario, the researcher has made a novel attempt to fill the gap. A research model has been proposed to fill up the research gap.

Methodology and Data Collection

CHAPTER III

Methodology and Data Collection

3.1 INTRODUCTION

This chapter deals with the methodology adopted for the present research study. It describes the design, sample, tools used, procedure of data collection and statistical techniques used for data analysis.

3.2 METHOD OF RESEARCH

The current research work is both descriptive and analytical. It is descriptive because the researcher is describing the lifestyle of women civil police officers in Kerala. Their work-life balance, job commitment, job satisfaction and overall life satisfaction is described in this study. Hence, the research design is descriptive. Since the study uses the statistical methods for analysing the quantitative data, it can be defined as an analytical study also.

3.2.1 Sources of Data

Both the secondary and primary data have been collected and used for the research work.

a. Primary Data

Primary data has been collected from women civil police offices in Kerala.

b. Secondary Data The secondary data needed for the study has been collected from the following sources:

- Data on police organisation published by Bureau of Police Research & Development
- Police Website
- A report published by women conferences
- Research Dissertations and Thesis
- Report published by police associations
- Police magazines

- Research Journals

- Periodicals

- Study Reports

- Research Publications

- Books related to the study area and

- Other websites

3.2.2 Sample Design

The sample design of the present research work is described in detail as follows:

3.2.3 Population

The population of the study comprises of women civil police officers in Kerala. Currently, there are 2404 women civil police officers working in 19 Police Districts in Kerala.

3.2.4 Population of WCPOs in police districts

The sample frame of the study consists of the total women civil police officers working in Kerala. The researcher selected 257 women civil police officers in the following manner.

Table 3.1:   Number of Women Civil Police Officers in North Zone under Thiruvananthapuram Range

Police Districts	Number of Women civil police Officers			Total
	Local Police Station	Women Police Station	Women Cell	
Thiruvananthapuram City	111	12	2	125
Thiruvananthapuram Rural	140	-	2	142
Kollam City	80	10	2	92
Kollam Rural	85	-	2	87
Pathanamthitta	53	-	2	55
Total	**469**	**22**	**10**	**501**

Source: Compiled from official websites of Kerala Police and the handbook of Kerala Police at a Glance

Table 3.2: Number of women civil police officers in North Zone under Ernakulam Range

Police Districts	Number of Women Civil Police Officers			Total
	Local Police Station	Women Police Station	Women Cell	
Alappuzha	-	15	2	17
Kottayam	149	17	2	168
Idukki	107	-	2	109
Kochi City	165	31	2	198
Ernakulam Rural	151	-	2	153
Total	**572**	**63**	**10**	**645**

Source: Compiled from official websites of Kerala Police and Kerala Police at Glance

Table 3.3: Number of Women Civil Police Officers in South Zone under Thrissur Range

Police Districts	Number of Women civil police Officers			Total
	Local Police Station	Women Police Station	Women Cell	
Thrissur City	45	9	2	56
Thrissur Rural	81	19	2	102
Palakkad	193	-	2	195
Malappuram	196	-	2	198
Total	**515**	**28**	**10**	**553**

Source: Compiled from official websites of Kerala Police and Kerala Police at Glance

Table 3.4: Number of women civil police officers in South Zone Under Thrissur Range

Police Districts	Number of Women Civil Police Officers			Total
	Local Police Station	Women Police Station	Women Cell	
Kozhikode City	144	24	2	170
Kozhikode Rural	122	-	2	124
Wayanad	66	-	2	68
Kannur	227	25	2	254
Kasaragod	87	-	-	87
Total	646	49	10	705

Source: Compiled from official websites of Kerala Police and Kerala Police At Glance

3.2.5 Sampling Technique

The sampling method followed is a probability-sampling method. The sampling technique is proportionately stratified sampling techniques.

The Table 3.5 shows the population size women civil police officers in each range.

Table 3.5: Number of Women Civil Police Officers

S.No.	Range	Number of WCPOs
1	TVPM	501
2	EKM	645
3	TSR	553
4	KNR	705
5	Total	2404

10% of the sample is selected from each range. Thus, the sample size is decided as follows.

Table 3.6: Sample Profile

S.No.	Range	Selected WCPOs in Each Range
1	TVPM	53
2	EKM	64
3	TSR	62
4	KNR	78
5	**Total**	**257**

3.2.6 Sample Unit

Women civil police officers are the sample units

3.2.7 Method of Data Collection

The first-hand information was collected through a well-structured questionnaire under direct oral investigation from women civil police officers on the constructs under study.

The questionnaire starts with demographic details of respondents, followed by questions relating to motivation factors attracted to the profession, parent demand, household responsibility, family support, work life, workplace support, work-life balance, organisational affective commitment, job satisfaction, and life satisfaction.

3.3 METHOD OF ANALYSIS FOLLOWED AND VARIABLES USED

The current study aims to study the work-life balance of women civil police officers in Kerala. It also covers antecedents and outcomes of work-life balance. To fulfil these objectives, the following constructs are used.

a) Motivation to join the profession

b) Parental and Household responsibility (Family Life/Family Demand)

c) Work Life (Job Demand/Work Challenges/ Job Characteristics)

d) Work-Life Balance

e) Family Support

f) Departmental Support

g) Superior Support

h) Co-worker Support

i) Job commitment

j) Job Satisfaction

k) Life Satisfaction

The scaling technique was used to convert the qualitative data into quantitative one. In this study, the researcher used a five-point Liker's scale the measuring instrument.

The Constructs used in the study are explained briefly as follows:

a) Motivation to join the profession

The researcher developed a scale for measuring the factors that motivated to enter the profession. It was designed by reviewing various studies related to career motivation and by discussing with the supervisor and officers in this field. 12 variables are identified. All the statements are positively worded, starting from 1 (Strongly Disagree) to 5 (Strongly Agree). After conducting Factor Analysis, three dimensions of motivational factors are identified. They are passion towards law enforcement, manliness, and security.

The following are the sub-variables used for measuring each dimension of motivation to join the profession

Table 3.7: Motivation to Join the Profession

Sl. No.	Dependent Variable		Independent Variable
1	Passion towards law enforcement	1	The chance to fight crime
		2	The opportunity to help people
		3	The prestige of the occupation
		4	Excitement about the job
		5	A lifetime interest in law enforcement
2	Manliness	1	Relative or close friend is a police officer
		2	The desire to be part of a male-dominated occupation
3	Security	1	The security of the job
		2	The salary and added benefits of the job

b) Household or Family Responsibility (Family Life)

In the present study for fulfilling the objective of measuring two aspects of family life, the researcher has referred existing scales developed and reported by Hyman et al. (2003). The scale is used for measuring Household responsibility index. The original scale consists of six items assessing the degree of household responsibility. Small changes have been made to this scale and factors like cooking, cleaning and washing has been put under household chores and billing responsibility (electricity, water, Telephone, Banking transactions and so on,) has been added based on the pilot study. To measure the parent demand, another scale was developed based on the Walia (2012). The original scale consists of six items. The present study uses five items and adds other two items based on the pilot study. It was a five-point response scale ranging from 1 (always some else's responsibility) to 5 (always my responsibility). Higher means indicate higher levels of demand and responsibility.

Table 3.8: Family Life

Sl. No.	Dependent Variable		Independent Variable
1	Household Responsibility	1	Household Chores(Cooking, Cleaning, Washing]
		2	Grocery/ Vegetable Purchase
		3	Shopping
		4	Billing (Electricity, Water, Telephone, Banking transactions etc.,)
		5	Small household repairs
		6	Childcare
2	Parental Demand	1	Helping the children in their studies
		2	To drop and pick the children from School/tuitions/extra-curricular activities
		3	To take the child for an outing
		4	To attend parent-teacher meetings at school
		5	Elderly care
		6	Financial support
		7	Saving &Investment decision

c) Work Life

The researcher developed a scale for measuring the work life of Women Civil Police Officer. It was designed by reviewing various studies related to police work life and by discussing with the supervisor and officers in this field. 27 variables are identified under three dimensions. All the statements are positively worded, starting from 1 (Strongly Disagree) to 5 (Strongly Agree), higher means indicate a higher level of work-related challenges.

Table 3.9: Variables of Work Life

Sl. No.	Dependent Variable		Independent Variable
1	Work Demand/ Job Demand	1	Long working hours
		2	Work time uncertainty
		3	Night duty
		4	Continuous job without proper rest time
		5	Continuous job without leave
		6	Inflexible working time
		7	Job stress
		8	Difficulty in availing casual leave
		9	Difficulty in getting a day off
		10	Having to do job-related work at home even on Leave days
		11	Frequent special duties
		12	Work overload
		13	Job resultant health problems
		14	Compulsory overtime
		15	Frequent stay away from home
		16	Different variety of jobs in a day
		17	Working irrespective of environment climate without a proper safety(rain, heat and so on.)

Sl. No.	Dependent Variable		Independent Variable
2	Working Condition	1	My department gives women police an opportunity to participate in mainstream police job
		2	I don't get the equal power that my male colleagues get
		3	I have experienced prejudices, bias and negative attitudes in my department
		4	I have to work twice as hard to prove myself and to be accepted
		5	Women in policing are expected to behave by male police peer norms
		6	I have undergone some sexual harassment, comments, eve teasing, advances, looks, touching etc., in my department
		7	I feel that I am insecure in my workplace primarily at night
3	Social attitude	1	The political inference is more in my job
		2	The public considers women police as inferior(lower) to men
		3	I have faced problems from culprits(criminals)

d) Family Social Support

In the present study for fulfilling the objective of measuring family support, the researcher has referred existing scales developed and reported by King et al. (1995), Family Support Inventory for Workers. It contains a 29-item emotional sustenance subscale and a 15-item instrumental assistance subscale. Based on the above scale the researcher has developed a scale after the pilot study. The present study consists of 14 items, one item under instrument assistance and others under the emotional assistance. In support system is considered by the husband, children, parent, in-law, relative, and society. It was a five-point response scale ranging from 1 (strongly disagree) to 5 (strongly agree). The scale is worded positively, and higher means indicate higher levels of family social support.

Table 3.10: Variables of Family Social Support

Sl. No.	Dependent Variable		Independent Variable
1	Instrument Support	1	If I have to work extra/extended hours, I can count on someone in my family to take care of everything at home
2	Emotional Support	1	If I have a problem at work, I usually share it with my family members.
		2	Members of my family want me to enjoy my job
		3	My husband supports me emotionally when I am stressed because of my work
		4	My husband advises me for betterment at work
		5	My husband is very cooperative and understands my work pressure
		6	My children are very cooperative and understand my work pressure
		7	My in-laws are very cooperative and understand my work pressure
		8	My parents are very cooperative and understand my work pressure
		9	I have a good relationship with all my family members
		10	I get all support and love that I want from my family
		11	My profession is fully accepted by my family
		12	My relatives do not blame me for missing family functions or gatherings because of my work
		13	My profession is fully accepted by society

e) Department Support

In the present study for fulfilling the objective of measuring the department support, the researcher has adapted from existing scales to suit the context of the study.

This study used four items in seven items version of the Perceived Organizational Support measure by Eisenberger et al. (1986) and rephrased the initially evaluated support from organisation to support from the department. They are framed in five-point Likert scale, all the statement are worded positively and higher means indicate higher levels of Department Support.

Table 3.11: Variables of Department Support

Sl. No.	Dependent Variable	Independent Variable	
1	Department Support	1	My department values my contribution
		2	My department appreciates any extra effort from me.
		3	My department responds promptly to my complaints
		4	My department cares about my well-being.

f) Superior Support

In the present study for fulfilling the objective of measuring the Superior Support, the researcher has referred existing scales developed and reported by Hammer et al. (2009). Their original scale consisted of 14 items, designed to assess four dimensions of superior Support: FSSB consists of four types of family supportive supervisor behaviours: emotional support, instrumental support, role model behaviours and recognition of the strategic importance of work-family issues, also called proactive, creative work-family management. Based on that the researcher has developed seven items scale under three dimensions of superior support: emotional support, instrumental support, and recognition of the strategic importance of work-family issues or proactive, creative work-family management. Respondents reported on a 5-point scale, ranging from 1 (strongly disagree) to 5 (strongly agree). All statements are worded positively, and higher means indicate higher levels of superior support.

Table 3.12: Variables of Superior Support

Sl.No	Dependent Variable		Independent variable
1	Emotional support	1	My superior officers understand my family demands
		2	My superior officers help in balancing my work and non-work life
		3	I can trust and believe my superior officer
		4	I can work smoothly with my superior officers
2	Instrumental support	1	My superior officers allow me to alter my shift work time
		2	My superior officers allow early going and late coming to meet my emergency needs
3	Recognition of the strategic importance of work-life balance or Proactive, creative work-family management	1	My supervisor officers think about how the work in my department can be organised to jointly benefit employees and the department.

g) Perceived co-worker support

In the present study for fulfilling the objective of measuring the co-worker Support, the researcher has adopted a seven-item from existing scales by Ducharme and Martin (2000) to suit the context of the study and has added three items developed from a pilot study used to measure the emotional support dimension of co-worker support. Using a 5-point Likert scale, respondents were asked to indicate their level of agreement on a scale ranging from (1) strongly disagree to (5) strongly agree, about perceptions of co-worker work-life balance support. Items were specific to emotional and instrumental support, all statements are worded positively, and higher means indicate higher levels of superior support.

Table 3.13: Variables of co-worker Support

Sl. No.	Dependent Variable		Independent Variable	
1	Emotional support/ Affective Support	1	My co-workers really care about me	
		2	I feel appreciated by my co-workers	
		3	My co-workers are friendly to me	
		4	I can work smoothly with my superior officers	
		5	I can trust and depend on my co-workers	
		6	I can freely & openly communicate with my co-workers	
2	Instrumental support	1	My co-workers would fill in while I am absent	
		2	My co-workers are helpful in getting my job done	
		3	My co-workers give useful advice on job-related problems	
		4	My co-workers give useful advice on family problems	

h) Work-Life Balance

In the present study for fulfilling the objective of measuring work Life Balance, the scales were adapted from existing scales to suit the context of the study. The scale used for measuring work-life balance is Hayman J. (2005) 13-item scale adapted from an instrument developed and reported Fisher et al. (2003) and added three items from a pilot study used to measure work /personal life enhancement dimensions of work-life balance. Their original scale consisted of 19 items, designed to assess three dimensions of work-life balance: Work Interference with Personal Life (WIPL), Personal Life Interference with Work (PLIW), and Work/Personal Life Enhancement (WPLE). Hence the number of questions included in work-life balance constructed is 16. The scale is measured using a 5-point Likert-type scale ranging from 1 (strongly disagree) to 5 (strongly agree). The WPLE subscale is worded positively, and higher means indicate higher levels of perceived work-life balance. The items with higher means on the WIF and FIW are purported to indicate lower levels of work-life balance. The WPLE subscale is worded positively, and higher means indicate higher levels of perceived work-life balance.

The following are the sub-variables used for measuring each dimension of work-life balance.

Table 3.14: Variables of Work-Life Balance

Sl. No.	Dependent Variable		Independent Variable
1	Work interference with personal life (WIPL)	1	My personal life suffers because of work.
		2	I neglect personal needs because of work.
		3	My job makes my personal life difficult.
		4	I put personal life on hold for work.
		5	I miss my activities because of my work.
2	Personal Life Interference with Work (PLIW)	1	My personal life drains me of energy for work
		2	I am too tired to be effective at work.
		3	My work suffers because of my personal life.
		4	I find it hard to work because of personal matters.
3	Work/Personal Life Enhancement (WPLE)	1	My personal life gives me energy for my job.
		2	My job gives me energy to do my personal activities.
		3	I am in a better mood at work because of my personal life.
		4	I am in a better mood because of my job.
		5	At work I develop new skills and this helps me to be a better family member.
		6	In my family life I develop new skills and this helps me to work better
		7	I am able to balance my work and family responsibilities.

i) Organizational commitment.

In the present study for fulfilling the objective of measuring the organisational commitment, the researcher has adopted seven items from existing scales Meyer and Allen's (1990) to suit the context of the study. Their original scale consisted of 8 items; this study has removed one item based on the pilot study. Using a 5-point Likert scale, respondents were asked to indicate their level of agreement on a scale ranging from (1) strongly disagree to (5) strongly agree, about perceptions of co-worker work-life balance support. All statements are worded positively, and higher means indicate higher levels of affective organisational commitment.

Table 3.15: Variables of Job Commitment

Sl.No	Dependent Variable		Independent Variable
1	Affective Commitment	1	I would be very happy to spend the rest of my career with this department
		2	I enjoy discussing my department with people outside it
		3	I feel as if this departments problems are my own
		4	I don't think I could easily get attached to any other profession
		5	I do feel like 'part of the family' at my department
		6	I feel 'emotionally attached' to this department
		7	I do feel a strong of belonging to my department

j) Job Satisfaction

In the present study for fulfilling the objective of measuring job satisfaction, the researcher has adopted nine items and rephrased it from existing scales Paul E. Spector (1999) to suit the context of the study. Their original scale consisted of 36 items, nine dimensions to assess employee attitude about job and aspects of the job. The present study has used nine items from nine dimensions and added one item under the dimension of nature of work and four items are added based on the pilot study. Using a 5-point Likert scale, respondents were asked to indicate their level of agreement on a scale ranging from (1) strongly disagree to (5) strongly agree, about job satisfaction. All the statements used positively and higher score means indicate higher levels of job satisfaction.

Table 3.16: Variables of Job Satisfaction

Sl. No.	Dependent Variable		Independent Variable
1	Pay	1	I am satisfied with the salary I receive
2	Promotion	1	I am satisfied with the promotion chances I receive
3	Superior	1	I am satisfied with my Superior officers
4	Fringe Benefits	1	I am satisfied with the benefits I receive
5	Contingent Rewards (performance-based rewards)	1	I am satisfied with the recognition I receive
6	Operating Procedures (required rules and procedures	1	I am satisfied with the rules and procedures in my job
7	Co-worker	1	I like the people I work with
8	Nature of Work	1	I feel a sense of pride in doing my job
		2	I am satisfied with my working conditions
9	Communication	1	Communication seems good within this organisation
10	Self	1	I am satisfied with being a police officer.
		2	I am interested in coming to work every day
		3	If I had a choice to make again, I would choose the same profession
		4	I will recommend others to this profession

k) Life satisfaction

In the present study for fulfilling the objective of measuring the life satisfaction, the researcher has adopted five items from existing scales Diener et al. (1985) to suit the context of the study. Using a 5-point Likert scale, respondents were asked to indicate their level of agreement on a scale ranging from (1) strongly disagree to (5) strongly agree, about perceptions of coworker work-life balance support. All statements are worded positively, and higher means indicate higher levels of life satisfaction.

Table 3.17: Variables of Life Satisfaction

Sl. No.	Dependent Variable		Independent Variable
1	Life Satisfaction	1	In most ways, my life is close to my ideal
		2	The conditions of my life are excellent.
		3	I am satisfied with my life
		4	So far I have gotten the important things I want in life
		5	If I could live my life over, I would change almost nothing.

3.4 CONCEPTUAL MODEL

The conceptual model used in the study using the above-mentioned variables are as follows:

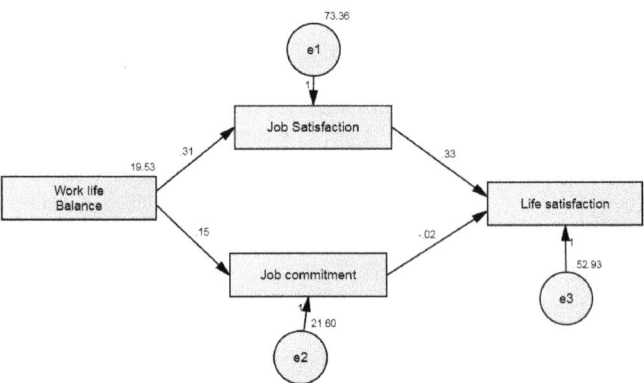

Figure 3.1: Conceptual Model

3.5 PILOT STUDY AND PRE-TEST

For finalising the scale, a pre-testing was done with 75 respondents. The experts in the field like academicians, experts, also crosschecked the questionnaire and officers in this field and their suggestions have been incorporated in it. After a pilot study, suitable modifications were incorporated into the questionnaire, and after that, the work of data collection was started.

3.6 RELIABILITY AND NORMALITY TESTING

For the scale evaluation, reliability and validity testing are generally applied.

A Reliability Testing

Reliability testing is essential for the validation of the scale. A measure is said to be reliable when it elicits the same response from the same person when the measuring instrument is administered to that person successively in similar or almost similar circumstances (Bajpai, 2011). In this study, the reliability of the measurement scales was tested using Cronbach's Alpha Reliability Coefficient.

Table: 3.18: Co-Efficient of the Constructs under Study

Sl No.	Constructs	X
1	Factors that attracted to the profession	0.877
2	Parental and household responsibilities	0.871
3	Work-life balance	0.833
4	Family support	0.901
5	Perception on job	0.854
6	Department support	0.833
7	Superior support	0.852
8	Co-worker support	0.912
9	Job commitment	0.862
10	Job satisfaction	0.912
11	Overall satisfaction	0.853

Reliability closer to unity (one) is right to say that tool/questionnaire will measure what is to be measured. Here reliability co-efficient ranging from 0.833 to 0.912 ensures questionnaire reliability.

Normality

To apply statistical tools to any data, data should ensure normality, i.e. the sample data should follow normal distributions. This is tested by judging equality of mean, median, mode, and Skewness closer to zero.

Table 3.19: Descriptive of the constructs under study

Descriptive	Profession	WLB	F.S	Perception	D.S.	S.S	C.S	J.C	J.S	L.S.
Mean	41.3658	55.9105	56.1673	90.4258	13.9689	23.6031	37.6498	24.4708	50.6926	39.9183
Median	43.0000	56.0000	56.0000	90.000	14.0000	24.0000	39.0000	25.0000	52.0000	40.0000
Mode	44.00	54.00	60.00	94.00	16.00	21.00	40.00	21.00	56.00	40.00
Std. Deviation	6.75661	8.02509	9.31351	16.36694	2.73129	4.60702	5.47597	4.70623	8.68968	7.81357
Skewness	-1.131	-.104	-.908	-.368	-.566	-.780	-.034	-.268	-1.151	-.318
Std. Error of Skewness	.152	.152	.152	.152	.152	.152	.152	.152	.152	.152
Kurtosis	1.150	.879	3.572	1.830	1.284	1.654	.313	1.674	3.124	.482
Std. Error of Kurtosis	.303	.303	.303	.303	.303	.303	.303	.303	.303	.303

3.7 TOOLS EMPLOYED FOR THE ANALYSIS OF DATA

From the above table, it is observed that for all the constructs mean median mode and Skewness is closer to zero. This indicates and ensures the normality of the data on which statistical tests can be applied

The tools used for the analysis are briefly discussed below.

a) Mean

The mean or average is a measure for representing the entire data by one value.

b) Percentages

In this study, the percentages are used for measuring the demographic variables.

c) Standard deviation

Standard deviation is used for measuring the deviation of values from the mean score.

d) 'Z' Test

It is used to determine whether there is any significant difference among the means of two independent groups. Linking demographic variable with antecedents and outcome of work-life balance.

e) One Way ANOVA

The One-way ANOVA stands for One-way Analysis of Variance (ANOVA). It is used to determine whether there is any significant difference among the means of three or more independent groups. This examines the association between demographic with antecedents and outcome of work-life balance.

f) Tukey HSD Post Hoc Test for Multiple Comparisons

Post hoc tests are designed for situations in which the researcher has already obtained a significant difference among three or more independent groups using ANOVA and to know the exact difference between these groups. Turkey HSD test is one of the most popular, conservative and flexible methods of post hoc test.

g) Factor Analysis

Factor analysis attempts to identify the underlying variables, or factors, that explain the pattern of correlation within a set of observed variables. It is useful for placing variables into meaningful categories. It is also used for identifying the most contributing dimensions. In this study, factor analysis has been executed to narrate the variable relating to motivation to choose police career.

h) Correlation Analysis

Correlation analysis is a technique used to measure the relationship between two quantitative variables. The Pearson Correlation coefficient is one of the methods used for finding out the correlation. The sample correlation coefficient value quantifies the strength and direction of the linear relationships. This study used to measure the relationship between the work-life balance, family support, perception of the job, department support, superior support, co-worker support, job commitment, job satisfaction, and life satisfaction.

i) Structural Equation Modeling (SEM)

SEM is used to develop a model to establish the independent and dependent relationship between the constructs under study.

The analysis of the quantitative data has been done with the help of statistical software called SPSS 17.

The Impact of Superior and Co-worker Support

CHAPTER 4

The Impact of Superior and Co-worker Support

4.1 INTRODUCTION

This chapter deals with the presentation and analysis of the data collected for the present study regarding the work particulars, personal profile, factors attracted to the profession, work-life balance, Family support, the Perception of the job, Department support, Superior support, Co-worker support, Job commitment, Job satisfaction, and Life Satisfaction. This offers a view of the summary of the data based on the constructs used in the study.

4.2 PROFILE OF WOMEN CIVIL POLICE OFFICERS

In order to do the analysis based on objectives, it is essential to examine the profile of the selected WCPOs.

a) **Zone-Wise Classification of WCPOs**

Table 4.1: Zone Wise Classification of Sample WCPOs

Zone	Number	Percentage
North	117	45.52
South	140	54.47
Total	**257**	**100**

Source: Primary Data

Table 4.1 shows the sector-wise classification of the sample chosen WCPOs.

Of the 257 WCPO taken for the analysis, 117 (45.52%) WCPO are from North zone, and 140 (54.47%) WCPO are from South zone.

b) **Range-wise Classification of WCPOs**

For administration, the geographical area of the state is bifurcated as South Zone and North Zone, which is headed by Additional Director General of Police. Further, each zone is divided into two ranges viz Thiruvananthapuram Range and Ernamkulam Range,

Thrissur Range and Kannur Range respectively. Again, the four ranges are divided into five districts each except Thrissur range. Thus, there are 19 police districts in Kerala. The state head of Kerala Police Force is State Police Chief, and he belongs to Director General of Police rank.

The officers of various ranks in ascending order is as follows Director General of Police and State Police Chief, Director General of Police, Additional Director General of Police, Inspector General of Police, Deputy Inspector General of Police, Superintendent of Police, Deputy Superintendent/Assistant Superintendent of Police, Inspector of Police, Sub-Inspector of Police, Assistant Sub-Inspector of Police, Senior Civil Police Officer/ Police Head Constable, Civil Police Officer/Police Constable All the four ranges and women civil police are selected as WCPO in the present study.

Table 4.2: Range Wise Classification of Sample WCPOs

Range	Number	Percentage
Thiruvananthapuram	53	20.62
Ernamkulam	64	24.90
Thrissur	62	24.12
Kannur	78	30.35
Total	**257**	**100**

Source: Primary Data

Table 4.2 reveals the WCPOs administrative range. 20.62%, 24.90% WCPOs from Thiruvananthapuram and Ernamkulum range respectively. 24.12%, in Thrissur range, and 30.35% WCPOs are from Kannur range.

c) Demographic Profile of the WCPOs

Table 4.3 represents the demographic profile of the sample WCPOs, which comprises the age, education, marital status, occupation of husband, type of family, total number of family member, total number of adult dependents, total number of child dependents, age of younger children, age of elder children, number of male children, number of female children, hours spend with family, monthly family income, residence type, service, working days, working hours, work schedule, travelling hours, time spending at work, award received and satisfaction with the infrastructure.

Table 4.3: Demographic Profile of WCPOs

Variables	Category	No. of WCPOs	Percentage
Age	18-30 years	52	20.2
	31-40 years	127	49.4
	41-50 years	52	20.2
	Above 51 years	26	10.2
	Total	**257**	**100**
Education Qualification	SSLC	39	15.2
	Pre-degree/Plus two	51	19.8
	Degree	112	43.6
	Postgraduate	55	21.4
	Total	**257**	**100**
Marital Status	Single	27	10.5
	Married	226	87.9
	Windows	4	1.6
	Total	**257**	**100**
Occupation of Husband	Same profession	25	9.8
	Govt. Job	107	41.6
	Pvt. Job	79	30.7
	Business	46	17.9
	Total	**257**	**100**
Type of Family	Joint	88	34.2
	Nuclear	168	65.8
	Total	**257**	**100**

Variables	Category	No. of WCPOs	Percentage
Number of Family Members	Up to 2 members	17	6.6
	3-5 members	230	89.5
	Above 6 members	10	3.9
	Total	**257**	**100**
Number of Adult Dependent	None	94	36.6
	1	44	17.1
	2	66	25.7
	More than 2	53	20.6
	Total	**257**	**100**
Number of Child Dependent	None	71	27.6
	1	63	24.5
	2	99	38.5
	More than 2	24	9.4
	Total	**257**	**100**
Age of Younger Child	Under 2 year	13	5.0
	2 to 5 years	50	19.4
	6 to 10 years	71	27.6
	Above 10 years	79	30.7
	N/A	44	17.3
	Total	**257**	**100**
Age of Elder Child	Under 2 year	17	6.6
	2 to 5 years	27	10.5
	6 to 10 years	70	27.2
	Above 10 years	111	43.1
	N/A	32	12.6
	Total	**257**	**100**

Variables	Category	No. of WCPOs	Percentage
Number of Male Children	Nil	101	39.3
	1-2	144	56.0
	More than 2	12	4.7
	Total	**257**	**100**
Number of Female children	Nil	81	35.4
	1-2	156	60.7
	More than 2	10	3.9
	Total	**257**	**100**
Hrs. spend with family	Less than 5 hours	94	36.6
	6 to 7 hours	104	40.5
	Above 7 hours	59	22.9
	Total	**257**	**100**
Monthly Family Income	Up to 40000	169	65.8
	40,001 to 60,000	76	29.6
	60,001 to 80,000	12	4.7
	Total	**257**	**100**
Residence Type	Rented House	16	6.2
	Own House	204	79.4
	Police Quarters	37	14.4
	Total	**257**	**100**
Service (years)	Below 5 years	41	16.0
	6 to 10 years	53	20.6
	11-15 years	129	50.2
	16 -20 years	34	13.2
	Total	**257**	**100**
Working days	6 days	97	37.7
	7 days	160	62.3
	Total	**257**	**100**

Variables	Category	No. of WCPOs	Percentage
Working Hours	8 – 9 hours	88	34.2
	9 -10 hours	46	17.9
	10 – 12 hours	83	32.3
	More than 12 hours	40	15.6
	Total	**257**	**100**
Work Schedule	General /Day Shift	58	22.6
	Night Shift	8	3.1
	Alternative Shift	191	74.3
	Total	**257**	**100**
Travelling Hours	Less than half an hour	79	30.7
	Nearly one hour	89	34.6
	Nearly two hours	58	22.6
	More than two hours	31	12.1
	Total	**257**	**100**
Time Spending at work	Very happy	29	11.3
	Happy	134	52.1
	Neutral	75	29.2
	Unhappy	16	6.2
	Very Unhappy	3	1.2
	Total	**257**	**100**
Award Received	Yes	86	33.5
	No	171	66.5
	Total	**257**	**100**
Satisfaction with the Infrastructure	Yes	128	49.8
	No	129	50.2
	Total	**257**	**100**

Source: Primary Data

Majority of the WCPOs (49.4%) are in the age group of 31-40, 20.2% WCPO is in the age group of 18-30 and 41- 50 years. Only 10.2% of the WCPOs are in the age group of 51 years.

About 43.6 % of WCPO have the graduation qualification, followed by post- graduation (21.4%), and pre-degree (19.8%). Only 15.2% of the WCPOs have SSLC qualification.

Married WCPOs comprise 87.9%, and WCPO of single status is only 10.5 %.

As far as the occupation of a spouse is concerned, 41.6% of spouse having have a government job, 30.7% in private job, 17.9% are businessmen and only 9.8 % work in the same profession.

Regarding the type of family, 65.8% of WCPOs live in a nuclear family, and WCPOs of joint family constitute 34.2 %.

Among 89.5% WCPOs family size is three to five members, 6.6 % have up to 2 members and only 3.9 % staying with six or more members.

36.6% of WCPOs do not have the responsibility of adult dependents. However, 25.7%, 20.6% and 17.1% WCPOs have two adults dependent, more than two adult dependent and one adult respectively. 38.5%, 24.5% and 9.4% WCPOs have a responsibility of two, one, and more than two children dependent responsibility. However, 27.62 WCPOs do not have child dependents.

About 30.7% of WCPOs have younger children who are above 10 years of age, followed by, 6 to 10 year aged children (27.6%), 19.4% WCOPs have children of 2-5 years of age, 17.3% of WOCPs do not have children and 5% of them have children of under 2 years.

About 43.1% of WCPOs have elder children who are above 10 years of age, followed by, 6 to 10 year aged children (27.2%), 12.6% of WCPOs do not have children, 10.5% WCOPs have 2-5 years of age children, 6.6% WOCPs have children of under 2 years.

56% of WCOPs have one or two male children, followed by 39.3% have no male children, 4.7% have more than two male children.

60.7% WCOPs have one or two female children, followed by 35.4% have no female child. And 3.9% have more than two female children.

Majority of WCPOs 40.5% spend time with their family only six or seven hours a day. 36.6 % and 22.9% spend less than five hours and more than 7 hours a day.

Monthly family income of WCPOs reveals that 65.8 % of the WCPOs earn up to Rs.40,000, 29.6 % of WCPO earn between Rs.40,001 to 60,000 and 4.7 % WCPOs earn between Rs.60,001 to 80,000.

79.4 % of WCPOs stay in their own house. 14.4 % only used police quarters the facility given by the department, remaining 6.2 % stay in the rented house.

The majority 50.2% of the WCPOs are of 11-15 years of service, 20.6 % of the WCPOs have under 6-10 year of service, 13.2 % WCPO under 16-20 years of service and remaining 16 % WCPO have less than 5 years in service.

Of the 62.3% of the WCPOs, 37.7% of WCPO work for six to seven days in a week.

Most of the WCPO work 34.2% in 8 or 9 hours, followed by 32.3% in 10 to 12 hours, 17.9% in 9 or 10 hours and 15.6% 12 hours respectively.

In the case of work schedule, 74.3% work in alternative shifts, which mean they work in day shift and night shift in rotation base. 22.6% work in general shift and 3.1% only work in night shifts.

34.6% of WCPO take 1-hour travel to reach their police station, 30.7% require less than half hours, 22.6% need two hours and 12.1% commuter more than two hours.

Majority of WCPOs 52.1% are happy about the time spend in their work, 29.2% of WCPOs express a neutral opinion, 11.3% WCPO opine very happy, 6.2% of WCPOs are unhappy and remaining 1.2% of WCPO are dissatisfied.

66.5% WCPOs have not received any award during their service, and 33.5% WCPO has received the award.

50.2% WCPO are satisfied with the infrastructure facility in the department, and 49.8% are not.

4.3 HOUSEHOLD RESPONSIBILITIES OF WCPOs

The responsibilities of the WCPOs are divided into two; one is household responsibilities and parental responsibilities.

Table 4.4 demonstrates on WCPOs time spend on take various household responsibilities for Cooking, cleaning and washing Grocery/ Vegetable purchase, for Shopping, to pay bills (Electricity, water, telephone, banking transactions and therefore, on), and small household repairs.

Cooking Cleaning and washing

113(44%) of WCOPs take 100% responsibilities for the Cooking Cleaning, and washing, followed by 67 (26.1%) take 75% responsibilities, 52 (20.2%) take 50% of work, 15(5.8%) take 25%, and only 10(3.9%) do not have any responsibility regarding cooking, cleaning and washing.

Grocery/ Vegetable purchase

61(23.7%) of WCOPs take 100% responsibilities for the grocery/vegetables purchase, followed by 60 (23.3%) take 75% responsibilities, 61 (23.7%) take 50% of work, 44(17.1%) take 25%, and only 31(12.2%) do not have any responsibility regarding grocery/ vegetable purchase.

Shopping

61(23.7%) of WCOPs take 100% responsibilities for shopping, followed by 70 (27.2%) take 75% responsibilities, 68 (26.5%) take 50% of work, 45(17.5%) take 25%, and only 13(5.1%) do not have any responsibility regarding shopping.

Pay bills

59 (23%) of WCOPs take 100% responsibilities for bill payment, followed by 52(20.2%) take 75% responsibilities, 56 (21.8%) take 50% of work, 59 (23 %) take 25%, and only 31(12 %) do not have any responsibility regarding bill payment.

Small Household Repairs

48 (18.7%) of WCOPs take 100% responsibilities for small household repairs, followed by 43 (16.7%) take 75% responsibilities, 58 (22.6%) take 50% of work, 68 (26.5 %) take 25%, and only 40(15.5%) do not have any responsibility regarding small household repairs.

Table 4.4: Household Responsibilities

Household responsibilities	Level of responsibilities	Number	Percentage
Cooking, Cleaning and Washing	100% own responsibility	113	44
	75 % own responsibility	67	26.1
	50 % own responsibility	52	20.2
	25% own responsibility	15	5.8
	100% others responsibility	10	3.9
	Total	**257**	**100**
Grocery/Vegetables purchase	100% own responsibility	61	23.7
	75 % own responsibility	60	23.3
	50 % own responsibility	61	23.7
	25% own responsibility	44	17.1
	100% others responsibility	31	12.2
	Total	**257**	**100**
Shopping	100% own responsibility	61	23.7
	75 % own responsibility	70	27.2
	50 % own responsibility	68	26.5
	25% own responsibility	45	17.5
	100% others responsibility	13	5.1
	Total	**257**	**100**
Billing(Electricity, Water, Telephone, Banking transactions etc.,)	100% own responsibility	59	23.0
	75 % own responsibility	52	20.2
	50 % own responsibility	56	21.8
	25% own responsibility	59	23.0
	100% others responsibility	31	12.0
	Total	**257**	**100**
Small household repairs	100% own responsibility	48	18.7
	75 % own responsibility	43	16.7
	50 % own responsibility	58	22.6
	25% own responsibility	68	26.5
	100% others responsibility	40	15.5
	Total	**257**	**100**

Source: Primary Data

4.4 PARENTAL RESPONSIBILITIES OF WCPOs

Table 4.5 demonstrates on WCPOs time spend on take various parental responsibilities for child care, helping the children in their studies, to drop and pick the children from school/tuitions/extracurricular activities, to take child outing, to attend parent-teacher meeting, elderly care, financial support and saving and investment decision.

Table 4.5: Parental Responsibilities

Parental responsibilities	Level of responsibilities	Number	Percentage
Child care	100% own responsibility	90	35.0
	75 % own responsibility	77	30.0
	50 % own responsibility	42	16.3
	25% own responsibility	16	6.2
	100% others responsibility	4	1.6
	Not Applicable	28	10.9
	Total	**257**	**100**
Helping the children in their studies	100% own responsibility	85	33.1
	75 % own responsibility	48	18.7
	50 % own responsibility	57	22.2
	25% own responsibility	21	8.2
	100% others responsibility	13	5.1
	Not Applicable	33	12.8
	Total	**257**	**100**
To drop and pick the children from school/tuitions/extracurricular activities	100% own responsibility	34	**13.2**
	75 % own responsibility	27	**10.5**
	50 % own responsibility	55	21.4
	25% own responsibility	44	17.1
	100% others responsibility	33	12.8
	Not Applicable	64	24.9
	Total	**257**	**100**

Parental responsibilities	Level of responsibilities	Number	Percentage
To take child outing	100% own responsibility	37	14.4
	75 % own responsibility	49	19.1
	50 % own responsibility	68	26.5
	25% own responsibility	37	14.4
	100% others responsibility	17	6.6
	Not Applicable	49	19.1
	Total	**257**	**100**
To attend parent teacher meeting	100% own responsibility	78	30.4
	75 % own responsibility	42	16.3
	50 % own responsibility	62	24.1
	25% own responsibility	24	9.3
	100% others responsibility	10	3.9
	Not Applicable	41	16.0
	Total	**257**	**100**
Elderly Care	100% own responsibility	57	22.2
	75 % own responsibility	47	18.3
	50 % own responsibility	73	28.4
	25% own responsibility	34	13.2
	100% others responsibility	10	3.9
	Not Applicable	36	14.0
	Total	**257**	**100**
Financial Support	100% own responsibility	64	24.9
	75 % own responsibility	78	30.4
	50 % own responsibility	84	32.7
	25% own responsibility	17	6.6
	100% others responsibility	14	5.4
	Total	**257**	**100**

Parental responsibilities	Level of responsibilities	Number	Percentage
Saving & Investment decision	100% own responsibility	68	26.5
	75 % own responsibility	63	24.5
	50 % own responsibility	86	33.5
	25% own responsibility	22	8.6
	100% others responsibility	18	7.0
	Total	**257**	**100**

Source: Primary Data

Child Care

90 (35%) of WCPOs take 100% responsibilities for child care, followed by 77(30.0%) take 75% responsibilities, 42 (16.3%) take 50% of work, 16 (6.2 %) take 25%, and only 4(1.6 %) do not have any responsibility regarding child care. 28(10.9%) WCPOs the situation does not arise.

Helping the children in their studies

85 (33.1%) of WCPOs take 100% responsibilities for helping the children in their studies, followed by 48(18.7%) take 75% responsibilities, 57 (22.2%) take 50% of work, 21 (8.2 %) take 25%, and only 13(5.1 %) do not have any responsibility regarding helping the children in their studies. 33(12.8%) WCPOs the situation does not arise.

Drop and pick the children from school/tuitions/extracurricular activities

34 (13.2%) of WCPOs take 100% responsibilities for drop and pick the children from school/tuitions/extracurricular activities, followed by 27(10.5%) take 75% responsibilities, 55 (21.4%) take 50% of work, 44 (17.1%) take 25%, and only 33(12.8 %) do not have any responsibility regarding for drop and pick the children from school/tuitions/extracurricular activities. 64(24.9%) WCPOs the situation does not arise.

Take child outing

37 (14.4%) of WCPOs take 100% responsibilities for taking child outing, followed by 49 (19.1%) take 75% responsibilities, 68(26.5%) take 50% of work,

37 (14.4%) take 25%, and only 17(6.6%) do not have any responsibility regarding child outing. 49(19.1%) WCPOs the situation does not arise.

Attend parent-teacher meeting

78 (30.4%) of WCPOs take 100% responsibilities to attend parent-teacher meeting, followed by 42 (16.3%) take 75% responsibilities, 62(24.1%) take 50% of work, 24 (9.3%) take 25%, and only 10(3.9%) do not have any responsibility regarding attending parent-teacher meeting. 41(16.0%) WCPOs the situation does not arise.

Elderly care

57 (22.2%) of WCPOs take 100% responsibilities for elderly care, followed by 47 (18.3%) take 75% responsibilities, 73(28.4%) take 50% of work, 34 (13.2%) take 25% , and only 10(3.9%) do not have any responsibility regarding elderly care. 36(14%) WCPOs the situation does not arise.

Financial support

64 (22.2%) of WCPOs take 100% responsibilities for financial support, followed by 78 (30.4%) take 75% responsibilities, 84(32.7%) take 50% of work, 17 (6.6%) take 25%, and only 14(5.4%) do not have any responsibility regarding financial support.

Saving and investment decision

68 (26.5%) of WCPOs take 100% responsibilities for saving, and investment decision, followed by 63 (24.5%) take 75% responsibilities, 86(33.5%) take 50% of work, 22(8.6%) take 25%, and only 18(7.0%) do not have any responsibility regarding saving and investment decision.

4.5 OPINION OF THE WCPOs ON THE CONSTRUCTS

The z test is used for comparing the opinion of the WCPOs on the construct Factors attracting to the profession, Work-life balance, Family support, Perception of the job, Department support, Superior support, Co-worker support, Job commitment, Job satisfaction and Life satisfaction concerning the following variables.

a) Marital status

b) Family type

c) Number of the male children

d) Number of female children

e) Number of days worked in a week

f) Work schedule

g) Award received

h) Infrastructure

i) Zones

j) Police station

a) Marital Status and Opinion on Constructs

Null Hypothesis: Both single and married WCPOs give on a same average level of opinion on the construct Factors attracting to the profession, Work-life balance, Family support, Perception of the job, Department support, Superior support, Co-worker support, Job commitment, Job satisfaction and Life Satisfaction.

Alternative Hypothesis: Both single and married WCPO give different level of opinion on the construct Factors attracting to the profession, Work-life balance, Family support, Perception of the job, Department support, Superior support, Co-worker support, Job commitment, Job satisfaction and Life Satisfaction.

Table 4.6: Marital Status and Opinion on Constructs

Constructs	Marital Status	Mean	z value	P value	Remark
Factors Attracting Profession	Single	43.778	1.576	0.116	Not significant
	Married	40.9735			
WLB	Single	53.2222	1.1781	0.076	Not significant
	Married	56.0841			
Family support	Single	55.5185	0.361	0.718	Not significant
	Married	56.2080			
Perception of job/ Work-life	Single	91.5926	0.464	0.643	Not significant
	Married	90.0444			
Department support	Single	13.8889	0.151	0.880	Not significant
	Married	13.9735			
Superior support	Single	25.3704	2.153	0.032**	Significant
	Married	23.3584			
Co-worker Support	Single	39.1111	1.434	0.153	Not significant
	Married	37.5088			
Job commitment	Single	23.4074	1.224	0.222	Not significant
	Married	24.5796			
Job satisfaction	Single	49.3333	.848	.397	Not significant
	Married	50.8363			
Life satisfaction	Single	39.7778	0.078	0.938	Not significant
	Married	39.9027			

Source: Primary Data

** Significant at 5% level

Table 4.6 shows that p-value is greater than 0.05, the level of significance for the constructs Factors attracting profession, Work-life balance, Family support, Perception of the job, Department support, Co-worker support, Job commitment, Job satisfaction and Life satisfaction

Therefore, in these cases (constructs) null hypothesis is accepted, and it is concluded that single and married WCPO experience same level of opinion on the Factors attracting profession, Work-life balance, Family support, Perception of the job, Department support, Co-worker support Job commitment, Job satisfaction and Life Satisfaction.

However, in the case of superior support p-value is less than 0.05, the level of significance. In this case, the null hypothesis is rejected. Moreover, it is concluded that the single and married WCPOs differ in their opinion on superior support.

By comparing the mean values, it is concluded that single WCPOs experience higher level of superior support.

b) Family Type and Opinion on Constructs

Null Hypothesis: Both joint and nuclear family WCPOs give on a same average level of opinion on the constructs Factors attracting to the profession, Work-life balance, Family support, Perception of the job, Department support, Superior support, Co-worker support, Job commitment, Job satisfaction and Life satisfaction.

Alternative Hypothesis:: Both joint and nuclear family WCPOs give different level of opinion on the constructs Factors attracting to the profession, Work-life balance, Family support, Perception of the job, Department support, Superior support, Co-worker support, Job commitment, Job satisfaction and Life satisfaction.

Table 4.7: Family Type and Opinion on Constructs

Constructs	Family type	Mean	Z Value	Sig.	Remark
Factors Attracting Profession	Joint Family	41.3864	.150	.881	Not significant
	Nuclear Family	41.2121			
WLB	Joint Family	51.8182	.058	.954	Not significant
	Nuclear Family	55.7576			
Family support	Joint Family	55.4545	.843	.400	Not significant
	Nuclear Family	56.4970			
Perception of job	Joint Family	92.7841	1.840	.067	Not significant
	Nuclear Family	88.8292			
Department support	Joint Family	14.2386	1.164	.245	Not significant
	Nuclear Family	13.8182			
Superior support	Joint Family	23.7386	.415	.678	Not significant
	Nuclear Family	23.4846			
Co-worker Support	Joint Family	37.7273	.100	.920	Not significant
	Nuclear Family	37.6545			
Job commitment	Joint Family	24.8977	1.094	.275	Not significant
	Nuclear Family	24.2182			
Job satisfaction	Joint Family	51.4041	.979	.328	Not significant
	Nuclear Family	50.2848			
Life satisfaction	Joint Family	39.3523	.799	.425	Not significant
	Nuclear Family	40.1758			

Source: Primary Data

** Significant at 5% level

Table 4.7 shows that p-value is found to be greater than 0.05, the level of significance for the all the constructs, i.e., Factors attracting profession, Work-life balance, Family support, Perception of the job, Department support, Superior support, Co-worker support, Job commitment, Job satisfaction and Life satisfaction

Therefore, in these cases (constructs) null hypothesis is accepted and it is concluded that all the WCPO living in the joint and nuclear family experience same level of opinion on Factors attracting profession, Work-life balance, Family support, Perception of job, Department support, Superior support, Co-worker support, Job commitment, Job satisfaction and Life Satisfaction.

c) Number of Male Children and Opinion on Constructs

Null Hypothesis: Both WCPO who have one or two male children and not having a male children give on a same average level of opinion on the construct Factors attracting profession, Work-life balance, Family support, Perception of job, Department support, Superior support, Co-worker support, Job commitment, Job satisfaction and   Life Satisfaction.

Alternative Hypothesis: Both WCPO who are having one or two male childrearing and not having a male children and give different level of opinion on the construct Factors attracting profession, Work-life balance, Family support, Perception of job, Department support, Superior support, Co-worker support, Job commitment, Job satisfaction and Life Satisfaction.

Table 4.8: Number of Male Children and Opinion on Constructs

Constructs	Number of male children	Mean	z Value	P Value	Remarks
Factors Attracting Profession	Nil	41.7647	.895	.372	Not significant
	1-2	40.6875			
WLB	Nil	56.4000	.585	.559	Not significant
	1-2	55.7847			
Family support	Nil	55.9882	.787	.432	Not significant
	1-2	56.9236			
Perception of job	Nil	86.6588	3.112	.002**	Significant
	1-2	93.3846			
Department support	Nil	14.0941	.580	.563	Not significant
	1-2	13.8819			
Superior support	Nil	23.5882	.403	.688	Not significant
	1-2	23.8403			
Co-worker Support	Nil	37.6353	.192	.848	Not significant
	1-2	37.5000			
Job commitment	Nil	23.2235	3.203	.002**	Significant
	1-2	25.1944			
Job satisfaction	Nil	48.5294	2.836	.005**	Significant
	1-2	51.8194			
Life satisfaction	Nil	39.6000	.409	.683	Not significant
	1-2	40.0486			

Source: Primary Data

**significant at 5% level.

Table 4.8 shows that p-value is greater than 0.05, the level of significance for the construct Factors attracting profession, Work-life Balance, Family support, Department support, Superior support, Co-worker support, and Life Satisfaction.

Therefore, in these cases (constructs) null hypothesis is accepted and it is concluded that all the WCPO who have one or two male children and not having a male children experience the same level of opinion on Factors attracting profession, Work-life balance, Family support, Department support, Superior support, Co-worker support, and Life Satisfaction

However, in the case of perception of the job, Job commitment, and Job satisfaction P-value is less than 0.05, the level of significance. Therefore, in this case, the null hypothesis is rejected. Moreover, it is concluded that the WCPO who have one or two male children and not having male children give different level of opinion on the construct like the perception of the job, Job commitment and Job satisfaction

By comparing the mean values, it is concluded that WCPO those who have one to two male children experience a higher level of Job commitment, Job satisfaction, and intricacies in the perception of the job,

d) Number of the female children and opinion on constructs

Null Hypothesis: Both WCPO who have one or two female children and not having a female children and give on an average same level of opinion on the construct Factors attracting profession, Work-life balance, Family support, Perception of job, Department support, Superior support, Co-worker support, Job commitment, Job satisfaction and Life Satisfaction.

Alternative Hypothesis: Both WCPO who have one or two female children and not having a girl child and give different level of opinion on the construct such as Factors attracting profession, Work-life balance, Family support, Perception of job, Department support, Superior support, Co-worker support, Job commitment, Job satisfaction and Life Satisfaction.

Table 4.9: Number of Female Children and Opinion on Constructs

Constructs	Number of female children	Mean	Z value	P value	Remarks
Factors Attracting Profession	Nil	43.3571	2.625	.009**	Significant
	1-2	40.0513			
WLB	Nil	53.4571	3.570	.000**	Significant
	1-2	57.2500			
Family support	Nil	54.7571	2.086	.038**	Significant
	1-2	57.3782			
Perception of job	Nil	89.3143	1.412	.159	Not significant
	1-2	92.5161			
Department support	Nil	13.9714	.616	.539	Not significant
	1-2	14.1987			
Superior support	Nil	24.2000	.412	.681	Not significant
	1-2	23.9359			
Co-worker Support	Nil	37.8429	.222	.825	Not significant
	1-2	37.6795			
Job commitment	Nil	25.1571	.947	.344	Not significant
	1-2	24.5385			
Job satisfaction	Nil	51.4429	.324	.746	Not significant
	1-2	51.0641			
Life satisfaction	Nil	39.8000	.187	.852	Not significant
	1-2	40.0128			

Source: Primary Data

**significant at 5% level

Table 4.9 shows that p-value is greater than 0.05, the level of significance for the constructs Department support, Superior support, Co-worker Support, Perception of the job, Job commitment, Job satisfaction and Life Satisfaction.

Therefore, in these cases (constructs) null hypothesis is accepted and it is concluded that all the WCPO who are having one or two female children and not having a female children experience the same level of opinion on Department support, Superior support, Co-worker Support, Perception of job, Job commitment, Job satisfaction and Life Satisfaction.

However, in the case of Factors attracting profession, Family support, and Work-life balance p-value is less than 0.05, the level of significance. Therefore, in this case, the null hypotheses are rejected.Moreover, it is concluded that the WCPO who are having one or two female children and not having a girl child give different level of opinion on the constructs such as Factors attracting profession, Family support and Work-life balance.

By comparing the mean values, it is concluded that WCPO those who have one or two female children experience a higher level of Work-life balance and Family support.

e) Number of days working in a week and opinion on constructs

Null Hypothesis: Both WCPOs work six days to seven days in a week give on a same average level of opinion on the constructs Factors attracting profession, Work-life balance, Family support, Perception of the job, Department support, Superior support, Co-worker support, Job commitment, Job satisfaction, and Life Satisfaction.

Alternative Hypothesis: Both WCPOs work six days to seven days in a week give different level of opinion on the constructs Factors attracting profession, Work-life balance, Family support, Perception of the job, Department support, Superior support, Co-worker support, Job commitment, Job satisfaction and Life Satisfaction.

Table 4.10: Number of Days Working in a Week and Opinion on Constructs

Constructs	Working days	Mean	z value	P value	Remarks
Factors Attracting Profession	6 days	41.6907	.463	.644	Not significant
	7 days	41.1688			
WLB	6 days	55.6701	.373	.709	Not significant
	7 days	56.0563			
Family support	6 days	56.4742	.411	.682	Not significant
	7 days	55.9813			
Perception of job	6 days	87.9588	1.893	.059	Not significant
	7 days	91.9308			
Department support	6 days	14.0619	.424	.672	Not significant
	7 days	13.9125			
Superior support	6 days	23.8557	.684	.495	Not significant
	7 days	23.4500			
Co-worker Support	6 days	37.8969	.563	.574	Not significant
	7 days	37.5000			
Job commitment	6 days	23.9794	1.305	.193	Not significant
	7 days	24.7688			
Job satisfaction	6 days	50.0515	.921	.358	Not significant
	7 days	51.0813			
Life satisfaction	6 days	41.1237	1.936	.054	Not significant
	7 days	39.1875			

Source: Primary Data

** Significant at 5% level

Table 4.10 shows that p-value is greater than 0.05, the level of significance for the all the constructs, i.e.,Factors attracting profession, Work-life balance, Family support, Perception of the job, Department support, Superior support, Co-worker support, Job commitment, Job satisfaction and Life satisfaction

Therefore, in these cases(constructs) null hypothesis is accepted and it is concluded that all the WCPOs working six days and seven days in a week experience same level of opinion on Factors attracting profession, Work-life balance, Family support, Perception of job, Department support, Superior support, Co-worker support, Job commitment, Job satisfaction and Life Satisfaction.

f) Work Schedule and opinion on constructs

Null Hypothesis: Both WCPOs work in day shift and alternative shift give on a same average level of opinion on the constructs Factors attracting profession, Work-life balance, Family support, Perception of the job, Department support, Superior support, Co-worker support, Job commitment, Job satisfaction and Life Satisfaction.

Alternative Hypothesis:: Both WCPOs work in day shift and alternative shift give different level of opinion on the constructs Factors attracting profession, Work-life balance, Family support, Perception of the job, Department support, Superior support, Co-worker support, Job commitment, Job satisfaction and Life satisfaction.

Table 4.11: Work Schedule and Opinion on Constructs

Constructs	Work Schedule	Mean	z value	P value	Remarks
Factors Attracting Profession	General/Day Shift	42.4310	1.041	.299	Not significant
	Alternative shift	41.0471			
WLB	General/Day Shift	57.7241	1.722	.086	Not significant
	Alternative shift	55.6859			
Family support	General/Day Shift	57.2414	.927	.355	Not significant
	Alternative shift	55.9529			
Perception of job	General/Day Shift	90.5965	.290	.772	Not significant
	Alternative shift	89.8901			
Department support	General/Day Shift	14.7414	2.493	.013**	significant
	Alternative shift	13.7330			
Superior support	General/Day Shift	23.9483	.626	.532	Not significant
	Alternative shift	23.5131			
Co-worker Support	General/Day Shift	38.7931	1.657	.099	Not significant
	Alternative shift	37.4555			
Job commitment	General/Day Shift	25.3276	1.638	.105	Not significant
	Alternative shift	24.1832			
Job satisfaction	General/Day Shift	50.5690	.222	.824	Not significant
	Alternative shift	50.8586			
Life satisfaction	General/Day Shift	41.6034	1.759	.080	Not significant
	Alternative shift	39.6021			

Source: Primary Data

** Significant at 5 %level.

Table 4.11 shows that p-value is greater than 0.05, the level of significance for the constructs, i.e. Factors attracting profession, Work-life balance, Family support, Perception of the job, Superior support, Co-worker support, Job commitment, Job satisfaction and Life satisfaction

Therefore, in these cases (constructs) null hypothesis is accepted, and it is concluded that all the WCPOs work in general and alternative shift experience the same level of opinion on Factors attracting profession, Work-life balance, Family support, Superior support, Department support, Co-worker support, and Life Satisfaction.

However, in the case of Department, support p-value is less than 0.05, the level of significance. Therefore, in this case, the null hypothesis is rejected. Moreover, it is concluded the WCPO working in the general shift and night have the difference in their opinion on Department support.

By comparing the mean values,, it is concluded that WCPOs those who are working in general shift experience higher level of support from their department

g) Award received and opinion on constructs

Null Hypothesis: Both awards received and not received WCPOs give on a same average level of opinion on the constructs Factors attracting profession, Work-life balance, Family support, Perception of the job, Department support, Superior support, Co-worker support, Job commitment, Job satisfaction and Life satisfaction.

Alternative Hypothesis: Both WCPOs who have received awards received and those who have not received award give different level of opinion on the constructs Factors attracting profession, Work-life balance, Family support, Perception of the job, Department support, Superior support, Co-worker support, Job commitment, Job satisfaction and Life satisfaction.

Table 4.12: Award Received and Opinion on Constructs

Constructs	Award received	Mean	t value	P value	Remarks
Factors Attracting Profession	Yes	42.0469	1.243	.215	Not significant
	No	40.6899			
WLB	Yes	54.7891	2.249	.025**	Significant
	No	57.0233			
Family support	Yes	57.4297	2.180	.030**	Significant
	No	54.9147			
Perception of job	Yes	89.9528	.456	.647	Not significant
	No	90.8915			
Department support	Yes	14.7734	4.912	.000**	Significant
	No	13.1705			
Superior support	Yes	24.2946	4.761	.000**	Significant
	No	22.2946			
Co-worker Support	Yes	37.9844	.976	.330	Not significant
	No	37.3178			
Job commitment	Yes	25.3359	2.580	.003**	Significant
	No	23.6124			
Job satisfaction	Yes	52.5469	3.481	.001**	Significant
	No	48.8527			
Life satisfaction	Yes	40.4453	1.077	.282	Not significant
	No	39.3953			

Source: Primary Data

** significant at 5% level

Table 4.12 shows that p-value is greater than 0.05, the level of significance for the constructs such as Factors attracting profession, Perception of the job, Co-worker Support and Life Satisfaction

Therefore, in these cases (constructs) null hypothesis is accepted, and it is concluded that the entire award received and not received WCPOs experience same level of opinion on Factors attracting profession, Perception of the job, Co-worker support, and Life Satisfaction.

However, in the case of Work-life balance, Family support, Department support, Superior support, Job commitment, and Job satisfaction p-value is less than 0.05, the level of significance. Therefore, in this case, the null hypothesis is rejected. Moreover, it is concluded that the award received and not received WCPO have a different level of opinion on Work-life balance, Family support, Department support, Superior support, Job commitment and Job satisfaction.

By comparing the mean values, it is concluded that WCPO those who received award showed a higher level of Family support, Department support, Superior support, Job commitment, and Job satisfaction.

h) Infrastructure and opinion on constructs

Null Hypothesis: Both Infrastructures satisfied and dissatisfied WCPO give on a same average level of opinion on the constructs Factors attracting profession, Work-life balance, Family support, Perception of the job, Department support, Superior support, Co-worker support, Job commitment, Job satisfaction and Life satisfaction.

Alternative Hypothesis: Both Infrastructures satisfied and dissatisfied WCPO give different level of opinion on the constructs Factors attracting profession, Work-life balance, Family support, Perception of the job, Department support, Superior support, Co-worker support, Job commitment, Job satisfaction and Life Satisfaction.

Table 4.13: Infrastructure and Opinion on Constructs

Constructs	Infrastructure	Mean	z value	P value	Remarks
Factors Attracting Profession	Yes	40.0930	1.658	.099	Not significant
	No	42.0056			
WLB	Yes	56.2326	.456	.649	Not significant
	No	55.7485			
Family support	Yes	56.4651	.363	.717	Not significant
	No	56.0175			
Perception of job	Yes	88.8721	1.081	.281	Not significant
	No	91.2118			
Department support	Yes	14.2209	1.049	.295	Not significant
	No	13.8421			
Superior support	Yes	24.3372	1.820	.070	Not significant
	No	23.2339			
Co-worker Support	Yes	38.86605	2.540	.012**	**Significant**
	No	37.0409			
Job commitment	Yes	25.3488	2.136	.034**	**Significant**
	No	24.0292			
Job satisfaction	Yes	52.4070	2.261	.025**	**Significant**
	No	49.8304			
Life satisfaction	Yes	40.48884	.829	.408	Not significant
	No	39.6316			

Source: Primary Data

**significant at 5 % level

Table 4.13 shows that p-value is greater than 0.05, the level of significance for the constructs, Factors attracting profession, Work-life balance, Family support, the perception of the job, Department support, Superior support, Co-worker support, Job commitment and Job satisfaction and Life Satisfaction.

Therefore, in these cases (constructs) null hypothesis is accepted, and it is concluded that all the infrastructure satisfied and dissatisfied WCPO experience the same level of opinion on Factors attracting profession, Work-life balance, Family support, the perception of the job, Department support, Superior support, and Life Satisfaction.

However, in the case of Co-worker support, Job commitment, and Job satisfaction p-value are less than 0.05, the level of significance. Therefore, in this case, the null hypotheses are rejected.Moreover, it is concluded that all the infrastructure satisfied and dissatisfied WCPO give a different level of opinion on Co-worker support, Job commitment and Job satisfaction.

By comparing the mean values, it is concluded that WCPO those who are satisfied with infrastructure shows a higher level of Co-worker support, Job commitment, and Job satisfaction.

i)   Zones and Opinion on Constructs

Null Hypothesis: Both WCPOs working under south and north zone give on a same average level of opinion on the constructs Factors attracting profession, Work-life balance, Family support, Perception of the job, Department support, Superior support, Co-worker support, Job commitment, Job satisfaction and Life satisfaction

Alternative Hypothesis: Both WCPOs working under south and north zone give different level of opinion on the constructs Factors attracting profession, Work-life balance, Family support, Perception of the job, Department support, Superior support, Co-worker support, Job commitment, Job satisfaction and Life satisfaction

Table 4.14: Zones and Opinion on Constructs

Constructs	Zones	Mean	T-test	P-value	Remarks
Attraction Factors	South	41.0902	.479	.632	Not significant
	North	41.6148			
WLB	South	55.8689	.079	.937	Not significant
	North	55.9481			
Family support	South	56.2787	.182	.856	Not significant
	North	56.0667			
Perception of job	South	91.8678	1.337	.183	Not significant
	North	89.1333			
Department support	South	13.8607	.603	.547	Not significant
	North	14.0667			
Superior support	South	23.1885	1.374	.171	Not significant
	North	23.9778			
Co-worker Support	South	37.4344	.599	.550	Not significant
	North	37.8444			
Job commitment	South	24.3770	.303	.762	Not significant
	North	24.5556			
Job satisfaction	South	50.5410	.265	.791	Not significant
	North	50.8296			
Life satisfaction	South	38.8279	2.142	.033**	Significant
	North	40.9037			

Source: Primary Data

** significant at 5 %level

Table 4.14 reveals that p-value is greater than 0.05, the level of significance for the constructs such as Factors attracting profession, Work-life balance, Family support, Department support, Superior support, Coworker support, the Perception of the job, Job commitment and Job satisfaction.

However, in these cases (constructs) null hypothesis is accepted and it is concluded that all the WCPOs working under south and north zone experience the same level of opinion on Factors attracting profession, Work-life balance, Family support, Department support, Superior support, Co-worker support, the Perception of the job, Job commitment and Job satisfaction.

However, in the case of Life satisfaction, the p-value is less than 0.05, the level of significance. Therefore, in this case, the null hypotheses are rejected. Moreover, it is concluded that the WCPOs working under south and north zone give different level of opinion on Life satisfaction.

Comparing the mean values, it is concluded that WCPOs those who are working in north zone showed more Life satisfaction.

j) Police station and opinion on constructs

Null Hypothesis: Both WCPOs working under local police station and Women police station give on a same average level of opinion on the constructs Factors attracting profession, Work-life balance, Family support, Perception of the job, Department support, Superior support, Co-worker support, Job commitment, Job satisfaction and Life satisfaction.

Alternative Hypothesis: Both WCPOs working under local police station and Women police station give different level of opinion on the constructs Factors attracting profession, Work-life balance, Family support, Perception of the job, Department support, Superior support, Co-worker support, Job commitment, Job satisfaction and Life satisfaction.

Table 4.15: Police Station and Opinion on Constructs

Constructs	Police station	Mean	t test	P-value	Remarks
Attraction factors	Local Police Station	41.2247	.565	.573	Not significant
	Women police Station	41.9394			
WLB	Local Police Station	55.3090	1.376	1.170	Not significant
	Women police station	56.8939			
Family support	Local Police Station	56.5169	.464	.643	Not significant
	Women police station	55.9394			
Perception of job	Local Police Station	90.0960	.257	.797	Not significant
	Women police station	90.6970			
Department support	Local Police Station	13.7921	1.191	.235	Not significant
	Women police station	14.2273			
Superior support	Local Police Station	23.6685	.211	.833	Not significant
	Women police station	23.5303			
Co-worker Support	Local Police Station	37.0899	.767	.444	Not significant
	Women police station	37.6667			
Job commitment	Local Police Station	24.3258	.225	.822	Not significant
	Women police station	24.1818			
Job satisfaction	Local Police Station	50.0337	1.521	.130	Not significant
	Women police station	51.8939			
Life satisfaction	Local Police Station	39.3652	1.266	.207	Not significant
	Women police station	40.8030			

Source: Primary Data

**Significant at 5% level

Table 4.15 finds that p-value is greater than 0.05, the level of significance for Factors attracting profession, Work-life balance, Family support, the Perception of the job, Department support, Superior support, Co-worker support, Job commitment and Job Satisfaction and Life Satisfaction.

However, in these cases (constructs) null hypothesis is accepted and it is concluded that all the WCPOs working in local police station and women police station experience same level of opinion on Factors attracting profession, Work-life balance, Family support, Perception of job, Department support, Superior support, Co-worker support, Job commitment and Job Satisfaction and Life satisfaction.

4.6 OPINION ON CONSTRUCTS (ANOVA)

One Way ANOVA test is used to test the demographic variables with the constructs Factors attracting profession, Work-life balance, Family support, the perception of the job, Department support, Superior support, Co-worker support, Job commitment, Job satisfaction and Life satisfaction.

a) Age

b) Educational Qualification

c) Spouse's Occupation

d) Number of Adult Dependent

e) Number of Child Dependent

f) Income

e) Age of Younger Child

g) Age of Elder Child

h) Time spend with family

i) Years of service's Experience

k) Working Hours

l) Travelling hours

a) Age

Comparing the opinion of WCPOs on the constructs under study with respect to age

Null Hypotheses: WCPOs belong to different age group give on an average (mean values are equal) same level of opinion on the constructs Factors attracting to the profession, Work-life balance, Family support, the perception of the job, Department support, Superior support, Co-worker support, Job commitment, Job satisfaction and Life satisfaction.

Alternative Hypothesis: WCPOs belong to different age group give (mean values are not equal)different level of opinion on the constructs Factors attracting to the profession, Work-life balance, Family support, the Perception of the job, Department support, Superior support, Co-worker support, Job commitment, Job satisfaction and Life satisfaction.

Table 4.16: Age wise Comparison with the Constructs under Study

Age	FAP	WLB	FS	PJ	DS	SS	CS	JC	JS	LS
					Mean					
18-30	42.9615	54.0000	54.9038	93.4661	13.6538	23.3462	37.1923	22.8269	47.9808	38.3654
31-40	40.9213	56.0236	56.1732	89.3413	13.6693	23.1890	37.4961	23.8268	49.3780	39.0472
41-50	39.8077	57.5192	57.3462	93.0385	14.4423	24.5769	38.5769	27.3654	55.4423	42.5385
Above 50	43.4615	55.9615	56.3077	84.3846	15.1154	24.1923	37.4615	25.1154	53.0385	42.0385
F Ratio	1.745	1.702	.596	2.444	2.848	1.317	.659	10.724	9.290	3.928
SIG	.158	.167	.618	.065	.038**	.269	.578	.000**	.000**	.009**
Remarks	Not Significant	Not Significant	Not Significant	Not Significant	Significant	Not Significant	Not Significant	Significant	Significant	Significant

Source: Primary Data

**Significant a5 5% level

For the constructs Factors attracting profession, Work-life balance, Family support, Perception of the job, Superior support and Coworker support p-value is greater than 0.05, the level of significance. Therefore, the null hypothesis is accepted, and it is concluded that WCPOs belong to different age group experience the same level of opinion on the constructs Factors attracting profession, Work-life balance, Family support, Perception of the job, Superior support, and Co-worker support.

For the constructs Department support, Job commitment, Job satisfaction and Life satisfaction p-value is less than 0.05, the level of significance. Therefore, the null hypothesis is rejected, and it is concluded that WCPOs belong to different age groups differ in their opinion Department support, Job commitment, Job satisfaction, and Life Satisfaction.

Post Hoc Test

ANOVA test finds that WCPOs belong to different age group differ significantly in their opinion on Job commitment, Job satisfaction, and Life Satisfaction

To find out which group differ significantly from others Tukey HSD Post-Hoc test is followed.

Table 4.17 : Age Group Significance on Constructs

Constructs	Age groups		Mean Difference	Significant
Job commitment	41 – 50 Yrs.	18- 30	4.5384*	.000
		31-40	3.5386*	.000
Job satisfaction	41 – 50 Yrs.	18- 30	7.4615*	.000
		31-40	6.0643*	.000
Life satisfaction	41 – 50 Yrs.	18- 30	4.1731*	.031
		31-40	3.4912*	.031

Source: Primary Data

*The mean difference is significant at 5% level

Tukey HSD Post Hoc test for Multiple Comparison in the case of job commitment, the result of Post Hoc test reveals that age group 41- 50 is significantly different from 18-30 and 31-40 with a mean difference of 4.5384 and 3.5386.

Regarding the Job satisfaction factor, 41-50 age group shows a significant difference between 18-30 and 31-40 with a mean difference of 7.4615 and 6.0643.

Table 4.17 shows that in case of Life satisfaction, there is a significant difference between the two age groups: 41-50 and 18-30 (mean difference 4.1731, P=.031).

In the case of Life satisfaction, the result of Post Hoc test reveals that age group 41- 50 is significantly different from 18-30 and 31-40 with a mean difference of 4.1731 and 3.4912.

Even though ANOVA indicate a significant difference in their opinion on department support but post-hoc concludes that there is no significant difference among any groups.

b) Education Qualification

Comparing the opinion of WCPOs on the constructs under study concerning Education Qualification

Null Hypotheses: WCPOs belong to different education qualification give on an average (mean values are equal) the same level of opinion on the constructs Factors attracting to the profession, Work-life balance, Family support, the perception of the job, Department support, Superior support, Co-worker support, Job commitment, Job satisfaction and Life satisfaction.

Alternative Hypothesis: WCPOs belong to different education qualification give (mean values are not equal) different level of opinion on the constructs Factors attracting to the profession, Work-life balance, Family support, the Perception of the job, Department support, Superior support, Co-worker support, Job commitment, Job satisfaction and Life satisfaction.

Table 4.18: Education wise Comparison with the Constructs under Study

Education Qualification	FAP	WLB	FS	PJ	DS	SS	CS	JC	JS	LS
	Mean									
SSLC	41.5897	57.4103	58.8205	93.1795	15.1026	24.7692	38.8974	27.3333	55.8462	42.0256
Pre-Degree	38.8627	55.5098	56.3137	87.9608	14.0980	23.7059	36.6275	24.2353	50.6667	38.3529
Degree	42.3036	55.9464	56.9911	91.8649	14.0714	23.5268	37.0357	24.9375	51.1518	39.4643
Post Gradate	41.6182	55.1455	52.4727	87.8545	12.8364	22.8364	38.9636	21.7091	46.1273	40.8000
F Ratio	1.859	.661	4.405	1.501	5.790	1.365	2.853	13.1788	10.863	2.011
Sig	.137	.577	.005**	.215	.001**	.254	.038**	.000**	.000**	.113
Remark	Not Significant	Not significant	Significant	Not significant	Significant	Not significant	Significant	Significant	Significant	Not significant

For the constructs Factors attracting profession, Work-life balance, Perception of the job, Superior support and Life satisfaction the p-value is greater than 0.05, the level of significance. Therefore, the null hypothesis is accepted, and it is concluded that WCPOs belong to the different category of education background show the same level of opinion on the constructs Factors attracting profession, Work-life balance, Perception of the job, Superior support, and Life satisfaction.

For the constructs Family support, Department support, Co-worker support, Job commitment and Job satisfaction the p-value is less than 0.05, the level of significance. Therefore the null hypothesis is rejected, and it is concluded that WCPOs belong to the different category of education background differ in their opinion Family support, Department support, Co-worker support, Job commitment and Job satisfaction.

Post Hoc Test

ANOVA test finds that WCPOs belong to different educational background significantly differ in their opinion on Family support, Department support, Job commitment, and Job satisfaction.

To find out which group differ significantly from others Post-Hoc test is carried out by using 'Tukey HSD' method.

Table 4.19: Educational Level Significance on Contracts

Constructs	Education level		Mean Difference	Significant
Family support	Postgraduate	SSLC	6.34779*	.006
		Degree	4.51834*	.015
Department support	Post graduate	SSLC	2.26620*	.000
		Degree	1.23506*	.026
Job commitment	SSLC	Pre-Degree	3.09804*	.006
		Degree	2.39583*	.019
		PG	5.62424*	.000
Job satisfaction	SSLC	Pre-Degree	5.1794*	.018
		Degree	4.6943*	.013
		PG	9.7188*	.000

Source: Primary Data
*The mean is significant at the 5% level

According to Table 4.19, Family support, Department support, Job commitment and Job satisfaction for the constructs the mean differences are significant. Since the p-value is less than 0.05, the level of significance. This reveals that WCPOs belong to the postgraduate, degree, and SSLC, give a significant opinion on Family support and Department support than the other education background group such as pre-degree.

However, in the case of Job satisfaction those who belong to the educational groups SSLC significantly different from 'pre-degree', 'degree', and 'postgraduate' with a mean difference of 5.1794, 4.6943, and 9.7188 respectively.

Similarly in the case of Job commitment those who are belong to the educational groups SSLC significantly different from 'pre-degree', 'degree', and 'postgraduate' with a mean difference of 3.09804, 2.39583 and 5.62424 respectively.

Even though ANOVA indicate a significant difference in their opinion on co-worker super but post-hoc concludes that there is no significant difference among any groups.

c) Spouse's Occupation

Comparing the opinion of WCPOs on the constructs under study with respect to Occupation of husband

Null Hypotheses: WCPOs belong to different category of spouse's occupation give on an average (mean values are equal) the same level of opinion on the constructs Factors attracting to the profession, Work-life balance, Family support, Perception of job, Department support, Superior support, Co-worker support, Job commitment, Job satisfaction and Life satisfaction

Alternative Hypothesis: WCPOs belong to different category of spouse's occupation give (mean values are not equal)different level of opinion on the constructs Factors attracting to the profession, Work-life balance, Family support, Perception of job, Department support, Superior support, Co-worker support, Job commitment, Job satisfaction and Life satisfaction.

Table 4.20: Comparison of Spouse's Occupation with the Constructs

Occupation of husband	FAP	WLB	FS	PJ	DS	SS	CS	JC	JS	LS
	Mean									
Same Profession	44.8000	57.5200	55.0000	89.3200	14.8800	24.4800	38.0400	24.2400	53.2400	41.7600
Govt.Job	41.1121	55.2897	57.0561	93.0189	14.0187	24.4766	37.7944	24.5140	51.7196	40.4393
Private Job	42.5063	55.7975	57.0633	89.9367	14.2025	22.9747	37.0000	25.0000	49.8608	40.0633
Business	38.1304	56.6739	53.1957	85.8913	12.9565	22.1739	38.2174	23.5870	48.3478	37.4565
F Ratio	3.986	.690	2.295	2.154	3.327	3.660	.660	.896	2.621	2.182
Sig	.008**	.559	.078	.094	.020**	.013**	.616	.444	.051	.091
Remarks	Significant	Not Significant	Not Significant	Not Significant	Significant	Significant	Not Significant	Not Significant	Not Significant	Not Significant

Source: Primary Data

** Significant at 5% level

For the constructs, Work-life balance, Family support, Perception of the job, Co-worker support, Job commitment, Job satisfaction and Life satisfaction p-value is greater than 0.05, the level of significance. Therefore, the null hypothesis is accepted, and it is concluded that WCPOs belong to the different category of spouse's occupation experience the same level of opinion on Work-life balance, Family support, Perception of the job, Co-worker support, Job commitment, Job satisfaction, and Life satisfaction.

For the constructs Factors attracting to the profession, Department support and Superior support the p-value is less than 0.05, the level of significance. Therefore, the null hypothesis is rejected, and it is concluded that WCPOs belong to the different category of spouses occupation differ in their opinion Factors attracting to the profession, Department support and Superior support.

To find out which group differ significantly from others Tukey HSD Post-Hoc test is followed.

Table 4.21: Occupational Groups Significance on Constructs

Constructs	Occupational Groups		Mean Difference	Significant
FAC	Business	Same Professional	6.66957*	.011
		Private Job	4.37589*	.033
Department support	Business	Same Professional	1.92348*	.023
Superior support	Business	Government Job	2.30272*	.022

Source: Primary Data

*The mean is significant at the 0.05 level

In the case of factors attracting profession, the result of Tukey HSD post hoc test, reveals that spouses occupation group business is significantly different from same profession and a private job with a mean difference of 6.66957 and 4.37589.

The test identifies that in the case of department support, spouse occupation group business is significantly different from the same profession with a mean difference of 1.92348.

Spouse occupational groups which are significantly different in the case of Superior support between business and government job with a mean difference of 2.30272.

d) Number of adult dependent

Comparing the opinion of WCPOs on the constructs under study with respect to the number of adult dependent

Null Hypotheses: WCPOs belong to different number of adult depended give on an average (mean values are equal) the same level of opinion on the constructs Factors attracting to the profession, Work-life balance, Family support, Perception of job, Department support, Superior support, Co-worker support, Job commitment, Job satisfaction and Life satisfaction.

Alternative Hypothesis: WCPOs belong to a different number of adult depended give (mean values are not equal) different level of opinion on the constructs Factors attracting to the profession, Work-life balance, Family support, the perception of the job, Department support, Superior support, Co-worker support, Job commitment, Job satisfaction and Life satisfaction.

Table 4.22: Comparison of Adult Dependent on the Constructs under Study

Number of Adult dependent	FAP	WLB	FS	PJ	DS	SS	CS	JC	JS	LS
	Mean									
None	39.4000	56.0375	57.1875	90.0253	13.5375	23.4125	38.4000	24.6375	49.6125	39.1500
1	41.7273	56.5000	55.0909	91.1818	14.2727	24.3636	37.8409	25.1591	53.7500	40.4773
2	43.1061	57.0152	56.0606	93.3182	14.0303	23.2879	36.4545	24.8788	Qw	40.2727
More than 2	42.7925	53.6981	56.4906	88.5660	14.3962	23.9623	37.5472	23.3019	50.8679	40.0189
F Ratio	2.703	1.871	.536	.949	1.343	.655	1.574	1.642	2.362	.363
Sig	.046**	.135	.658	.418	.261	.580	.196	.180	.072	.780
Remarks	Significant	Not Significant	Not Significant	Not Significant	Not Significant	Not Significant	Not Significant	Not Significant	Not Significant	Not Significant

Source: Primary Data

** Significant at 5% level

For the constructs, Work-life balance, Family support, Perception of the job, Department support, Superior support, Co-worker support, Job commitment, Job satisfaction and Life satisfaction the P-value is greater than 0.05, the level of significance. Therefore the null hypothesis is accepted, and it is concluded that WCPOs belong to a different number of adult dependent's group experience the same level of opinion Work-life balance, Family support, Perception of the job, Department support, Superior support, Co-worker support, Job commitment, Job satisfaction and Life Satisfaction. For the constructs Factors attracting to the profession, P-value is less than 0.05, the level of significance. Therefore the null hypothesis is rejected, and it is concluded that WCPOs belong to a different number of adult dependent differ in their opinion Factors attracting to the profession.

Even though ANOVA indicates a significant difference in their opinion factors attracting to the profession but post-hoc concludes that there is no significant difference among any group.

e) **Number of Child Dependent**

Comparing the opinion of WCPOs on the constructs under study with respect to the number of a Child dependent

Null Hypotheses: WCPOs belong to different number of child depended give on an average (mean values are equal) same level of opinion on the constructs Factors attracting to the profession, Work-life balance, Family support, Perception of job, Department support, Superior support, Co-worker support, Job commitment, Job satisfaction and Life satisfaction.

Alternative Hypothesis: WCPOs belong to different number of child depended give (mean values are not equal) different level of opinion on the constructs Factors attracting to the profession, Work-life balance, Family support, the Perception of the job, Department support, Superior support, Co-worker support, Job commitment, Job satisfaction and Life satisfaction.

Table 4.23: Comparison of Child Dependent with the Constructs under Study

Number of a child dependent	FAP	WLB	FS	PJ	DS	SS	CS	JC	JS	LS
	Mean									
None	42.2941	54.7647	56.3725	91.5294	13.6667	23.7647	35.9412	23.8824	49.3922	38.6275
1	41.3333	57.7143	55.5238	91.4127	14.5556	24.3810	39.4444	24.6667	52.1111	39.9048
2	39.9192	56.1818	56.7980	91.7245	13.6970	23.3232	37.2727	24.9091	50.3333	40.1919
More than 2	43.3333	56.2917	53.2917	88.0417	13.8750	22.8750	38.8333	24.7083	50.2917	38.6667
F Ratio	1.379	1.382	1.040	.348	1.469	.913	4.745	.526	.987	.587
Sig	.250	.249	.376	.790	.224	.435	.003**	.665	.399	.624
Remarks	Not Significant	Not Significant	Not Significant	Not Significant	Not Significant	Not Significant	Significant	Not Significant	Not Significant	Not Significant

Source: Primary Data

** Significant at 5% level

For the constructs Factors attracting profession, Work-life balance, Family support, Perception of job, Department support, Superior support, Job commitment, Job satisfaction and Life satisfaction p-value is greater than 0.05, the level of significance. Therefore the null hypothesis is accepted, and it is concluded that WCPOs belong to a different number of child dependent's group experience the same level of opinion constructs Factors attracting profession, Work-life balance, Family support, Perception of the job, Department support, Superior support, Job commitment, Job satisfaction and Life satisfaction.

For the constructs co-worker Support, the p-value is less than 0.05, the level of significance. Therefore the null hypothesis is rejected, and it is concluded that WCPOs belong to a different number of child dependent differ in their opinion on Co-worker support.

Post Hoc Test

ANOVA test finds that WCPOs belong to a different number of a child depended significantly differ in their opinion on Co-worker support.

To find out which group differ significantly from others Post-Hoc test is followed.

Table 4.24: Child Dependent Significance on Constructs

Constructs	Number of a child dependent		Mean difference	Significant
Co -worker Support	One	None	3.50327*	.003
		Two	2.17172	.055
		More than two	2.6111	.963

Source: Survey Data
* Significant at 5% level

The Co-worker support child dependent concerned; there is a significant difference between single child dependent and no dependent with a mean difference of 3.50327. The post hoc result demonstrated that there is no significant difference between one to two and one to more than two child dependent groups.

f) Income

Comparing the opinion of WCPOs on the constructs under study concerning Income

Null Hypotheses: WCPOs belong to different category of income group give on an average (mean values are equal) the same level of opinion on the constructs Factors attracting to the profession, Work-life balance, Family support, Perception of job, Department support, Superior support, Co-worker support, Job commitment, Job satisfaction and Life satisfaction

Alternative Hypothesis: WCPOs belong to the different category of income (mean values are not equal) different level of opinion on the constructs Factors attracting to the profession, Work-life balance, Family support, the Perception of the job, Department support, Superior support, Co-worker support, Job commitment, Job satisfaction and Life satisfaction.

Table 4.25: Comparison of Income with the Constructs

Income	FAP	WLB	FS	PJ	DS	SS	CS	JC	JS	LS
	Mean									
Up to 40000	41.1124	55.2071	55.2485	89.8988	13.5503	23.1361	38.3553	23.7160	49.2071	38.4142
40,001-60,000	42.3816	57.4605	57.3553	90.2763	14.8421	24.5000	36.0000	25.8421	53.2368	42.9342
60,001-80,000	38.5000	56.000	61.5833	98.7500	14.3333	24.5000	37.6498	26.4167	55.5000	42.0000
F Ratio	1.745	1.702	.596	2.444	2.848	1.317	.659	10.724	9.290	3.928
Sig	.158	.167	6.18	.065	.038**	.269	.578	.000**	.000**	.009**
Remarks	Not Significant	Not Significant	Not Significant	Not Significant	Significant	Not Significant	Not Significant	Significant	Significant	Significant

Source: Primary Data

** Significant at 5% level

For the constructs Factors attracting profession, Work-life balance, Family support, Perception of the job, Superior support and Co-worker support p-value is greater than 0.05, the level of significance. Therefore the null hypothesis is accepted, and it is concluded that WCPOs belong to the different category of income group experience the same level of opinion on Factors attracting profession, Work-life balance, Family support, Perception of the job, Superior support.

For the constructs Department support, Job commitment, Job satisfaction and Life satisfaction p-value is less than 0.05, the level of significance. Therefore the null hypothesis is rejected, and it is concluded that WCPOs belong to different categories of income group give different level of opinion on Department support, Job commitment, Job satisfaction and Life satisfaction.

Post Hoc Test

ANOVA test finds that WCPOs belong to different income group significantly differ in their opinion on Department support, Job commitment, Job satisfaction and Life satisfaction.

To find out which group differ significantly from others Tukey HSD Post-Hoc test is applied.

Table 4.26: Different Income Groups Significance on Constructs

Constructs	Different Income Groups		Mean Difference	Significant
Department support	40,001-60,000	Up to 40,000	1.2981*	.002
Job commitment	40,001-60,000	Up to 40,000	2.12613*	.003
Job satisfaction	Up to 40,00	40,001-60,00	4.02974	.002*
		60,001-80,000	6.29290	.036*
Life satisfaction	40,001-60,000	Up to 40,000	4.52001	.000*

Source: Survey Data

* Significant at 5% level

Table 4.26 shows that there are some income groups which are significantly different. The test identified the income group of Rs.40,001 -60,000 and up to Rs.40,000 which are significantly different in their Department support, Job commitment and Life satisfaction with a mean difference of 1.2981, 2.12613 and 4.52001 respectively.

Job satisfaction concerned the income group of Rs.40,000 is significantly different from   Rs.40,001 -60,000 and 60,001 to 80,000 with mean difference 4.02974 and 6.29290 respectively.

7. Age of Younger Child

Comparing the opinion of WCPOs on the constructs under study with respect to age of younger child

Null Hypotheses: WCPOs belong to different category age group of younger child give on an average (mean values are equal) same level of opinion on the constructs Factors attracting to the profession, Work-life balance, Family support, Perception of job, Department support, Superior support, Co-worker support, Job commitment, Job satisfaction and Life satisfaction.

Alternative Hypothesis: WCPOs belongs to different category age group of younger child   give (mean values are not equal) different level of opinion on the constructs Factors attracting to the profession, Work-life balance, Family support, Perception of job, Department support, Superior support, Co-worker support, Job commitment, Job satisfaction and Life satisfaction.

Table 4.27: Comparison of Age of the Younger Child with the Constructs under Study

Age of younger child	FAP	WLB	FS	PJ	DS	SS	CS	JC	JS	LS
					Mean					
Under 2	40.8462	55.5385	58.8462	99.6154	15.6923	25.8462	39.6923	26.2308	54.0769	41.3077
2 to 5 Years	40.8800	52.3000	53.9200	86.6200	13.7200	23.1000	37.5000	24.5600	48.4800	39.4200
6 to 10 Years	41.5634	57.7606	54.9718	89.2535	13.3803	22.3803	38.5211	23.6197	49.4789	39.2254
Above 10 Years	40.3924	57.6329	58.1266	91.6538	14.2025	24.2911	36.8228	24.9494	51.8481	40.2152
N/A	42.7000	55.3000	57.3000	91.1000	14.6333	24.8333	37.2000	25.0333	52.2333	40.9000
F Ratio	.425	5.383	2.243	1.912	2.906	3.196	1.488	1.307	2.250	.424
Sig	.790	.000**	.065	.109	.022**	.014**	.207	.268	.064	.791
Remarks	Not Significant	Significant	Not Significant	Not Significant	Significant	Significant	Not Significant	Not Significant	Not Significant	Not Significant

Source: Primary Data

** Significant at 5% level

For the constructs Factors attracting profession, Family support, Perception of the job, Coworker support, Job commitment, Job satisfaction Life satisfaction p-value is greater than 0.05, the level of significance. Therefore the null hypothesis is accepted, and it is concluding that WCPOs belong to a different category or various age group of younger child experiences the same level of opinion Factors attracting profession, Family support, Perception of the job, Co-worker support, Job commitment, Job satisfaction and Life satisfaction.

For the constructs of Work-life balance, Department support and Superior support the p-value is less than 0.05, the level of significance. Therefore the null hypothesis is rejected, and it is concluding that WCPOs belong to different age group of a younger child differ in their opinion on Work-life balance Department support and Superior support.

Even though ANOVA indicates a significant difference in their opinion on Work-life balance Department support and Superior support but post-hoc concludes that there is no significant difference among any group.

7. Age of Elder Child

Comparing the opinion of WCPOs on the constructs under study concerning the age of the elder child

Null Hypotheses: WCPOs belong to different category age group of elder child give on an average (mean values are equal) same level of opinion on the constructs Factors attracting to the profession, Work-life balance, Family support, Perception of job, Department support, Superior support, Co-worker support, Job commitment, Job satisfaction and Life satisfaction.

Alternative Hypothesis: WCPOs belong to different category age group of elder child number of child give (mean values are not equal) different level of opinion on the constructs Factors attracting to the profession, Work-life balance, Family support, Perception of job, Department support, Superior support, Co-worker support, Job commitment, Job satisfaction and Life satisfaction.

Table 4.28: Comparison of Age of Elder Child with the Constructs under Study

Age of elder child	FAP	WLB	FS	PJ	DS	SS	CS	JC	JS	LS
					Mean					
Under 2	46.2941	55.4706	53.7641	95.4706	14.4118	24.8235	37.5296	23.4118	52.8824	37.5882
2 to 5 Years	41.2593	54.1111	56.4815	93.9259	14.1111	24.8148	38.0370	22.6667	48.0370	39.8889
6 to 10 Years	40.4714	56.5714	54.7857	88.5857	13.5286	23.5000	37.7857	24.6429	49.5143	38.6286
Above 10 Years	40.6737	55.6396	58.0000	90.6091	14.2523	23.4865	37.0991	25.3063	52.0811	41.5315
N/A	36.0000	54.0000	54.0000	97.6667	13.000	22.6667	36.3333	20.6667	43.6667	39.6667
F Ratio	1.865	.503	1.850	1.117	1.003	.785	.310	2.827	2.535	2.086
Sig	.118	.734	.120	.349	.407	.536	.871	.026	.041	.084
Remarks	Not Significant	Not Significant	Not Significant	Not Significant	Not Significant	Not Significant	Not Significant	Significant	Significant	Not Significant

Source: Primary Data

**Significant at 5%

For the constructs Factors attracting profession, Work life balance, Family support, Perception of job Department support, Superior support, Co-worker support and Life satisfaction p-value is greater than 0.05, the level of significance. Therefore the null hypothesis is accepted, and it is concluded that women civil police officers belonging to the different category of the age group of elder child experience the same level of opinion on Factors attracting profession, Work life balance, Family support, Perception of job Department support, Superior support and Co-worker support and Life satisfaction.

For the constructs of Job commitment and Job satisfaction, the p-value is less than 0.05, the level of significance. Therefore, the null hypothesis is rejected, and it is concluding that women civil police officers various age group of an elder child differ in their opinion on Job commitment and Job satisfaction.

Even though ANOVA indicates a significant difference in their opinion on Job commitment and Job satisfaction but post-hoc concludes that there is no significant difference among any groups.

7. Time Spent with Family

Comparing the opinion of WCPOs on the constructs under study concerning time spent with family

Null Hypotheses: WCPOs belong to different hours spend with family give on an average (mean values are equal) the same level of opinion on the constructs Factors attracting to the profession, Work-life balance, Family support, perception of job, Department support, Superior support, Co-worker support, Job commitment, Job satisfaction and Life satisfaction.

Alternative Hypothesis: WCPOs belong to different hours spend with family give different (mean values are not equal) level of opinion on the constructs Factors attracting to the profession, Work-life balance, Family support, the Perception of the job, Department support, Superior support, Co-worker support, Job commitment, Job satisfaction and Life satisfaction.

Table 4.29: Comparison of Time Spent with Family and the Constructs under Study

Hours spend with family	FAP	WLB	FS	PJ	DS	SS	CS	JC	JS	LS
	Mean									
Less than 5 hrs	42.5745	56.7128	56.5213	90.5914	14.2766	23.7660	38.8299	25.6170	51.8511	39.0213
6 to 7 hrs	40.6731	56.2308	56.1250	90.7019	13.6923	23.2981	37.2308	23.5865	49.2308	40.5673
Above 7 hrs	38.7778	53.2222	56.3111	90.7778	13.9778	24.0667	36.9556	24.2222	51.1111	40.2000
F Ratio	4.00	2.135	.390	.337	.752	.362	3.002	3.229	1.775	.676
Sig	.008**	.096	.761	.799	.522	.780	.031**	.023**	.152	.586
Remarks	Significant	Not Significant	Not Significant	Not Significant	Not Significant	Not Significant	Significant	Significant	Not Significant	Not Significant

Source: Primary Data

**Significant at 5 % level.

For the constructs, Work-life balance, Family support, Perception of the job, Superior support, Department support, Job Satisfaction and Life Satisfaction p-value is greater than 0.05, the level of significance. Therefore, the null hypothesis is accepted, and it is concluded that WCPOs belong to the different category of hours spent with the family of experience the same level of opinion on Work-life balance, Family support, Perception of the job, Superior support, Department support, Job Satisfaction and Life satisfaction.

For the constructs on Factors attracting to the profession, Co-worker support, and Job commitment, the p-value is less than 0.05, the level of significance. Therefore, the null hypothesis is rejected, and it is concluded that WCPOs belong to the different category of hours spent with the family of experience differ in their opinion on Factors attracting to the profession, Co-worker support and Job commitment.

Even though ANOVA indicates a significant difference in their opinion on Factors attracting to the profession, Co-worker support and Job commitment but post-hoc concludes that there is no significant difference among any groups.

7. Years of Experience

Comparing the opinion of WCPOs on the constructs under study concerning years of experience

Null Hypotheses: WCPOs belong to different years of service give on an average (mean values are equal) the same level of opinion on the constructs Factors attracting to the profession, Work-life balance, Family support, Perception of job, Department support, Superior support, Co-worker support, Job commitment, Job Satisfaction and Life satisfaction.

Alternative Hypothesis: WCPOs belong to different years of service give different (mean values are not equal) level of opinion on the constructs Factors attracting to the profession, Work-life balance, Family support, the Perception of the job, Department support, Superior support, Co-worker support, Job commitment, Job Satisfaction and Life satisfaction.

Table 4.30: Comparison of Service with the Constructs under Study

Experience	FAP	WLB	FS	PJ	DS	SS	CS	JC	JS	LS
					Mean					
Below 5 years	42.3415	55.7561	56.3415	94.0732	13.7317	23.3171	37.9512	22.3902	49.0000	38.7317
6 to 10 years	43.6415	55.6226	54.6981	86.6415	13.9245	23.3208	36.2642	24.3585	50.2830	41.1509
11-15 years	40.0155	56.8140	55.3566	89.4688	14.0155	24.0465	38.5814	25.3235	51.3953	39.1550
16 to 20 years	41.7647	53.1176	61.3235	95.5294	14.1471	22.7059	35.9114	24.4708	50.7059	42.3235
F Ratio	2.450	1.967	4.414	2.936	.167	.947	3.670	3.613	.837	2.272
Sig	.064	.119	.005**	.034**	.919	.419	.013**	.014**	.474	.081
Remarks	Not Significant	Not Significant	Significant	Significant	Not Significant	Not Significant	Significant	Significant	Not Significant	Not Significant

Source: Primary Data

**Significant at 5% level

For the constructs Factors attracting profession, Work-life balance, Superior support, Department support, Job Satisfaction and Life Satisfaction p-value is greater than 0.05, the level of significance. Therefore, the null hypothesis is accepted, and it is concluded that WCPOs different years of service experience give the same level of the opinion the constructs Factors attracting profession, Work-life balance, Perception of the job, Superior support, Department support, Coworker support, Job commitment, Job Satisfaction and Life Satisfaction

For the constructs Family support, Perception of the job, Co-worker support, and Job commitment p-value are less than 0.05, the level of significance. Therefore, the null hypothesis is rejected, and it is concluded that WCPOs belong to different service experiences give different level of opinion on Family support, the Perception of the job, Co-worker support and Job commitment.

Post Hoc Test

From the ANOVA it is found that women civil police officers belonging to different service experiences give different level of opinion on Family support, the perception of the job, Co-worker support and Job commitment.

To find out which group differ significantly from others Post-Hoc test is carried out by using 'Tukey HSD' method

Table 4.31. Significantly Different Service Groups

Constructs	Years of Service		Mean Difference	Significant
Family Support	16-20 yrs	6 to 10 yrs	6.62542	.014
		11-15 yrs	5.96694	.010
Job Commitment	11- 15 yrs	Below 5	2.56324	.025

Table 4.31 shows the result of post hoc test for conducting the intergroup comparison. From the Tukey HSD post hoc test, it is clear that there are differences 16 to 20 years of service with and 6 to 10 years of service and 11 to 15 years with means difference of 6.62542 and 5.96694 in the case of a family. However, in the case of job commitment the significant difference between the group 11 to 15 years of service and below 5 with a mean difference of 2.56324.

Even though ANOVA indicates a significant difference in their opinion on the perception of the job and co-worker support but post-hoc concludes that there is no significant difference among any groups.

7. Working Hours

Comparing the opinion of WCPOs on the constructs under study concerning working hours

Null Hypotheses: WCPOs belong to different working hours give on an average (mean values are equal) the same level of opinion on the constructs Factors attracting to the profession, Work-life balance, Family support, the Perception of the job, Department support, Superior support, Co-worker support, Job commitment, Job Satisfaction and Life satisfaction.

Alternative Hypothesis: WCPOs belong to different working hours give different level of opinion on the constructs Factors attracting to the profession, Work-life balance, Family support, the Perception of the job, Department support, Superior support, Co-worker support, Job commitment, Job Satisfaction and Life satisfaction.

Table 4.32: Comparison of Working Hours with the Constructs under Study

Working Hours	FAP	WLB	FS	PJ	DS	SS	CS	JC	JS	LS
					Mean					
8-9 hrs	41.0341	55.1477	57.4205	89.9773	13.4318	22.9773	37.6498	23.6136	48.8182	41.1477
9-10 hrs	42.1522	55.5652	56.7174	93.0870	14.6304	24.0000	36.2727	25.3696	52.6304	38.9318
10-12 hrs	42.3494	55.6627	54.0120	88.0482	13.9636	23.4096	37.3133	23.9880	49.3253	39.5250
Above 12 hrs	39.1500	58.5000	57.2500	93.3590	14.5250	24.9250	40.0250	26.3250	55.4250	39.5250
F Ratio	1.375	1.722	2.280	1.436	2.653	1.819	5.445	4.032	7.264	1.152
Sig	.251	.163	.080	.233	.049	.144	.001	.008	.000	.329
Remark	Not Significant	Not Significant	Not Significant	Not Significant	Significant	Not Significant	Significant	Significant	Significant	Not Significant

Source: Primary Source

**Significant at 5% level

Table 4.32 observed are observed. For the constructs Factors attracting profession, Work-life balance, Family support, Perception of the job, Superior support, Job commitment and Life Satisfaction p-value is greater than 0.05, the level of significance. Therefore, the null hypothesis is accepted, and it is concluding that WCPOs belong to various working hours experience the same level of opinion on Factors attracting profession, Work-life balance, Family support, Perception of the job, Superior support and Life satisfaction.

For the constructs Department support, Co-worker Support, Job commitment, and Job satisfaction p-value is less than 0.05, the level of significance. Therefore, the null hypothesis is rejected, and it is concluded that WCPOs belong to different working hours give different level of opinion on Department support, Co-worker support, and Job satisfaction.

To find out which group differ significantly from others Tukey HSD Post-Hoc test is followed.

Table 4.33: Significantly Different Working hours Groups

Constructs	Number of working hours		Mean Difference	Significant
Co-worker Support	More than 12 hrs	8-9 hours	3.75227	.004**
Job Commitment	More than 12	8-9 hours	2.71136	.026**
Job Satisfaction	More than 12	8-9 hours	6.6668	.001**

Source: Primary Data
** Significant at 5% level

The test identified the more than 12 hours working WCPO is significantly different from 8 to 9 hours working WPO in the case of Co-worker support, Job commitment and Job satisfaction with the mean difference 3.75227, 2.71136 and 6.6668 respectively.

Even though ANOVA indicates a significant difference in department Support but post-hoc concludes that there is no significant difference among any groups.

7. Travelling from home to Workplace

Comparing the opinion of WCPOs on the constructs under study concerning travel hours from home to workplace

Null Hypotheses: WCPOs belong to different hours spend on travelling give on an average (mean values are equal) the same level of opinion on the constructs Factors attracting to the profession, Work-life balance, Family support, Perception of job, Department support, Superior support, Co-worker support, Job commitment, Job satisfaction and Life satisfaction.

Alternative Hypothesis: WCPOs belong to different hours spend on travelling working hours give (mean values are not equal) different level of opinion on the constructs Factors attracting to the profession, Work-life balance, Family support, Perception of job, Department support, Superior support, Co-worker support, Job commitment, Job satisfaction and Life satisfaction.

Table 4.34: Comparison of Travelling Hours with the Constructs under Study

Travelling Hours	FAP	WLB	FS	PJ	DS	SS	CS	JC	JS	LS
					Mean					
>1/2 hr	40.4684	41.3656	55.9105	88.3462	13.6835	23.4684	36.1266	24.1139	50.5316	50.6926
Nearly 1 Hr	39.5618	53.7595	57.0886	90.6629	14.1124	23.9888	38.3483	25.0225	51.6742	39.5316
Nearly two hrs	43.6379	57.5345	56.9310	95.3621	14.4310	24.3276	38.8793	24.4828	50.3793	39.4270
<2 Hrs	44.5806	60.1290	55.0645	85.7419	13.4310	21.4839	37.2258	23.7742	48.8710	39.6379
F Ratio	4.399	6.054	.828	3.106	1.347	2.962	3.668	.784	.865	1.663
Sig	.005**	.001**	.480	.027**	.260	.033**	.013**	.504	.460	.175
Remarks	Significant	Significant	Not Significant	Significant	Not Significant	Significant	Significant	Not Significant	Not Significant	Not Significant

Source: Primary Data

**Significant at 5 % level

From the above tables following observations are made for the constructs Family support, Department support, Job commitment, Job and Life Satisfaction p-value is greater than 0.05, the level of significance. Therefore, the null hypothesis is accepted, and it is concluding that WCPOs belong to various hours spend for travel to workplace experience the same level of opinion on Family support, Department support, Job commitment, Job and Life satisfaction.

For the constructs Factors attracting to the profession, Work-life balance, the Perception of the job, Superior support and Co-worker support p-value is less than 0.05, the level of significance. Therefore, the null hypothesis is rejected, and it is concluded that WCPOs belong to various hours spend for travel to workplace differ in their opinion on Factors attracting to the profession, Work-life balance, the Perception of the job, Superior support and Co-worker support.

Even though ANOVA indicates a significant difference in Factors attracting to the profession, Work-life balance, the perception of the job, Superior support and Co-worker support but post-hoc concludes that there is no significant difference among any groups.

4.7 INTERRELATIONSHIP BETWEEN THE CONSTRUCTS

This research aims in estimating the relationship between the construct and in proving the impact of Factors attracting profession, Work-life balance, Family support, Perception of the job, Department support, Superior support, Co-worker support, Job commitment, Job Satisfaction on the total Life satisfaction. Hence, correlation analysis is done to find out the interrelationship between constructs under study. The following Table 4.32 gives the correlation between the constructs.

Table 4.35: Inter-Correlation Matrix for the Construct under Study (N=257)

Constructs		FS	PJ	DS	SS	CS	JC	JS	WLB	LS
FS	R		.287	.333	.299	.135	.285	.280	.120	.335
	sig		.000**	.000**	.000**	.031**	.000**	.000**	.054	.000**
PJ	r	.288		.254	.280	.109	.252	.303	.092	.011
	sig	.000**		.000**	.000**	.082	.000**	.000**	.141	.861
DS	r	.333	.224		.581	.310	.490	.618	.177	.268
	sig	.000**	.000**		.000**	.000**	.000**	.000**	.004**	.000**
SS	r	.299	.280	.581		.280	.434	.521	.152	.145
	sig	.000**	.000**	.000**		.000**	.000**	.000**	.015**	.020**
CS	r	.135	.109	.310	.280		.348	.312	.290	.218
	sig	.013**	.082	.000**	.000**		.000**	.000**	.000**	.000**
JC	r	.285	.252	.490	.434	.348		.618	.145	.216
	sig	.000**	.000**	.000**	.000**	.000**		.000**	.020**	.001**
JS	r	.280	.303	.618	.521	.312	.618		.157	.360
	sig	.000**	.000**	.000**	.000**	.000**	.000**		.012**	.000**
WLB	r	.120	.092	.177	.152	.290	.145	.157		.192
	sig	.054	.141	.004**	.015**	.000**	.020**	.012**		.002**
LS	r	.335	.011	.268	.145	.218	.216	.360	.192	
	sig	.000**	.861	.000**	.020**	.000**	.001**	.000**	.002**	

Source: Primary Data; **Significant at 5 % level

The constructs Factors attracting profession, Work-life balance, Family support, Perception of the job, Department support, Superior support, Co-worker support, Job commitment, Job Satisfaction on the total Life satisfaction are related to each other.

It concludes that almost all the construct under study are significantly and positively corrected with each other.

4.8 FACTORS ATTRACTING THE WCPOS TOWARDS THEIR PROFESSION (FACTOR ANALYSIS)

This study aims to find the items/aspects that attracted the WCPOs to choose this profession. Twelve items were identified for this purpose. However, to find few important items from these items are difficult. Hence the data reduction method –factor analysis is followed to identify the latent constraints (factors) from these twelve items.

The following sections explain the factors analysis procedure to find the factors that influence the WCPOs to select this profession.

Table 4.36 gives Kaiser-Mayer-Oklin and Bartlett Tests. KMO value 8.876 closer to unity and significant value of Bartlett's test 0.000 ensures the application of factor analysis on the given the data.

Table 4.36: KMO and Bartlett's Test

Kaiser-Meyer-Olkin Measure of Sampling Adequacy		.876
Bartlett's Test of Sphericity	Approx. Chi-Square	1590.318
	Df	66
	Sig.	.000

Source: Primary Data

Table 4.37: Communalities

Items	Initial	Extraction
Excited about the job	1.000	.637
The Opportunity to Help People	1.000	.760
The Security of the Job	1.000	.660
The Salary and Added Benefits of the Job	1.000	.608
Relative or Close Friend being a Police Officer	1.000	.561
The Authority and Power Associated with the Job	1.000	.628
A Lifetime Interest in Law Enforcement	1.000	.688
Lack of Other Job Opportunities	1.000	.659
The Desire to be Part of a Male-Dominated Occupation	1.000	.568
The Chance to Fight Crime	1.000	.762
The Prestige of the Occupation	1.000	.707
The job is Different every day	1.000	.731

Source: Primary Data

Table 4.37 shows the Communalities values range from .568 to .762 which are reasonably closer one indicate all the items are significantly contributing to the factors under study.

Table 4.38 Total Variance Explained

Items	Initial Eigenvalues			Extraction Sums of Squared Loadings			Rotation Sums of Squared Loadings		
	Total	% of Variance	Cumulative %	Total	% of Variance	Cumulative %	Total	% of Variance	Cumulative %
1	5.53	46.106	46.105	5.533	46.106	46.106	4.783	39.190	39.190
2	1.422	11.847	57.953	1.422	11.847	57.953	1.871	15.595	54.784
3	1.015	8.456	66.409	1.015	8.456	66.409	1.395	11.625	66.409
4	.829	6.910	73.319						
5	.700	5.837	79.156						
6	.629	5.244	84.400						
7	.531	4.428	88.828						
8	.380	3.165	91.993						
9	.323	2.689	94.682						
10	.242	2.016	96.698						
11	.221	1.844	98.542						
12	.175	1.458	100.000						

Extraction Method: Principal Component Analysis

Table 4.38 the total variance explained is 66.409 % which is acceptable. Also, this indicates three factors are in the Table 4.39.

Component Matrix

Table 4.39: Rotated Component Matrix

Items	Component		
	1	**2**	**3**
12	.820	.233	.070
2	.816	-.073	.299
11	.806	.215	.108
10	.803	.331	.089
1	.782	.006	.159
7	.782	.272	.055
6	.701	.357	.097
8	-.034	.802	.121
5	.362	.656	-.023
9	.422	.615	-.106
3	.202	-.010	.787
4	.087	.053	.773

Source: Primary Source

The first factor is consisted by Job is different every day (12), opportunity to help people (2), the prestige of the occupation (11), chance to fight crime (10), excitement about the job (1), a lifetime interest in law enforcement (7) all these statement this factor can be named as **Passion towards Law Enforcement.**

The second factor is constituted by lack of other job opportunities (8) relative or friends being a police officer (5), the desire to part of a male-dominated occupation (9) this factor can be named as **Manliness.**

The third factor is the combination of security of the job (3) and salary and benefits (4) this factors cab be named as **Security.**

Thus it may be concluded that one is **Passion towards Law Enforcement** second one is **Manliness** and the third one is **Security** are the factors that attract the women civil police officers to this profession

4.9 RESEARCH MODEL ANALYSIS

This research attempts to analyse the influence of different factors influencing Work-life balance of WCPOs in Kerala. The study made an effort to prove the relationship between the different factors of Work-life balance.

The proposed research model developed for the study is given in Figure 4.1. In the research model, since all the constructs are related to each other to know the dependence and interdependence of these constructs the structured equation model is constructed. When the constructs play both independent and dependent variable roles, SEM is the suitable tool to establish the empirical relationship between them.

4.9.1 Model 1

The following model gives the relationship between Family support, co-worker support, Superior support (first stage independent variables) and Work-life balance (first stage dependent variable). Then the impact of Work-life balance on **Job Satisfaction** and Life Satisfaction is given

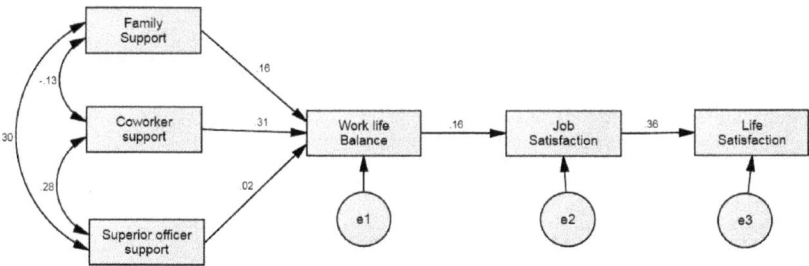

Figure 4.1: Research Model -1

Model Validity

To ensure the model validity the following indicates were checked

Chi-Square = 133.250, Degree of freedom =7, Probability=0.000, Goodness of Fit Index (GFI):0.871, Augmented Goodness of Fit (AGFI):0.614, Normative Fit Index NFT):0.797, Relative Fit Index (RFI):0.777, Incremental Fit Index IFI):0.711, Comparative Fit Index (CFI): 0.795, Roof Mean Square Error Approximately (RMSEA)=0.165.

All the fit indicates reasonably close to unity (one), and FMSEA closer to Zero indicates model Validity.

Table 4.40a gives the direct and indirect impact of the constructs under study.

Table 4.40a: Constructs Related

Constructs Related	Direct Effect	Indirect Effect
Family support and Work-life balance	0.16 (.155)	
Co-worker support and Work-life balance	0.31 (.305)	
Superior support and Work-life balance	0.020 (.020)	
Work-life balance and Job Satisfaction	0.160 (.157)	
Job Satisfaction and Life Satisfaction		0.024
Family support and Job Satisfaction		0.003
Superior support and Job Satisfaction		0.048
Co-worker support and Job Satisfaction	0.360 (.360)	0.009
Family support and Life Satisfaction		0.001
Superior support and Life Satisfaction		0.017
Co-worker support and Life Satisfaction		

Source: Primary Data

From the model, it is understood that taking the impact of Superior support, the Co-worker support influenced Work-life balance of the WCPOs, i.e. taking the impact of Superior support, the Co-worker Support influences Work-life balance to the extent of 31%.

Hence, it is interpreted that Superior support and Co-worker Support play a positive and significant role in the Work-life balance of the WCPOs. Also it worth to note that taking the impact of Superior support, the family also influenced the work-life balance of the WCPOs.

It is observed that the organisation recognises the family of the WCPOs and family of the WCPOs respect the organisation.

The net point is that Work-life balance influences Job Satisfaction to the extent of 16 % and Job Satisfaction influences Life Satisfaction to the extent of 36%. One unit improves this means of Work-life balance then 0.16 units will improve Job satisfaction and when One unit Life satisfaction improves job 0.36 units influence Satisfaction.

This implies that Work-life balance influence positively the Job Satisfaction and Life satisfaction of the WCPOs

4.9.2 Model 2

The following model gives the relationship between the constructs Family support, Coworker Support, Superior support, Work-life balance, Job commitment, and Life satisfaction.

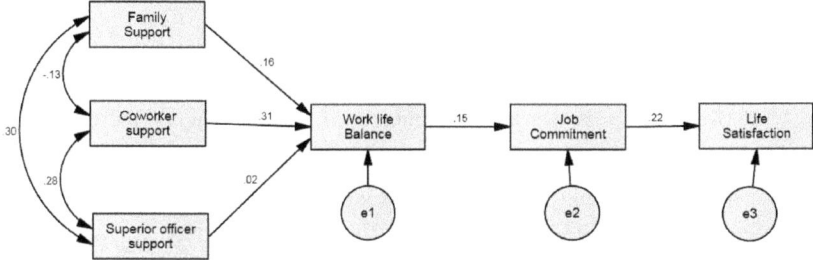

Figure 4.2: Research Model – 2

Model Validity

To ensure the model validity the following indicates are found

Chi-Square = 126.348, Degree of freedom =7, Probability=0.000, Goodness of Fit Index (GFI):0.880, Augmented Goodness of Fit (AGFI):0.639, Normative Fit Index

NFT):0.760, Relative Fit Index (RFI):0.758, Incremental Fit Index (IFI):0.744, Comparative Fit Index (CFI): 0.754, Roof Mean Square Error Approximately (RMSEA)=0.158.

All the fit indicates reasonably close to unity (one), and FMSEA closer to Zer0 indicates model Validity.

Table 4.40b gives the direct and indirect impact of the constructs under study.

Table 4.40b: Constructs Related

Constructs Related	Direct Effect	Indirect Effect
Family support and Work-life balance	0.16(0.155)	
Co-worker support and Work-life balance	0.31(0.305)	
Superior support and Work-life balance	0.02(0.020)	
Work-life balance and Job commitment	0.15(0.145)	
Job commitment and Life Satisfaction	0.22(0.216	
Superior support and Job commitment		0.003
Superior support and Life Satisfaction		0.003
Co-worker support and Job commitment		0.041
Co-worker support and Life Satisfaction		0.010
Family support Job commitment		0.023
Family support and Life Satisfaction		0.005

Source: Primary Data

This analysis finds that taking the impact of Superior support, the Co-worker support influences Work-life balance to the extent of 31%. Also taking the impact of Superior support, The Family support influences Work-life balance to the extent of 16%.

It is empirically proved that organisation recognises the WCPOs family and WCPOs family respect the organisation.

Also, it is observed that Work-life balance influences Job commitment to the extent of 16% and Job commitment influences Life satisfaction to the extent of 22%. This means that one unit in the improvement of Work-life balance lead to 0.16 unit improvement in Job commitment and one unit improvement in Job commitment will lead to 0.22 unit implement of Life satisfaction.

It is worth to note that Co-worker support and Family support indirectly influences Job commitment and Life Satisfaction. Family support and Co-worker support play a useful role in influencing Job commitment.

From the above correlation analysis and two models, it can be said that the WCPOs experience right amount of Family support, Co-worker support, Superior support which leads to Work-life balance. Their Work-life balance leads to Job Satisfaction and Job commitment. Finally, Work-life balance, Job Satisfaction, and Job commitment lead to overall Life satisfaction.

4.9.3 Model 3

Still, this research aims to find the impact of Work-life balance on Life satisfaction of the WCPOs through Job satisfaction and Job commitment. The following model exhibit this relationship.

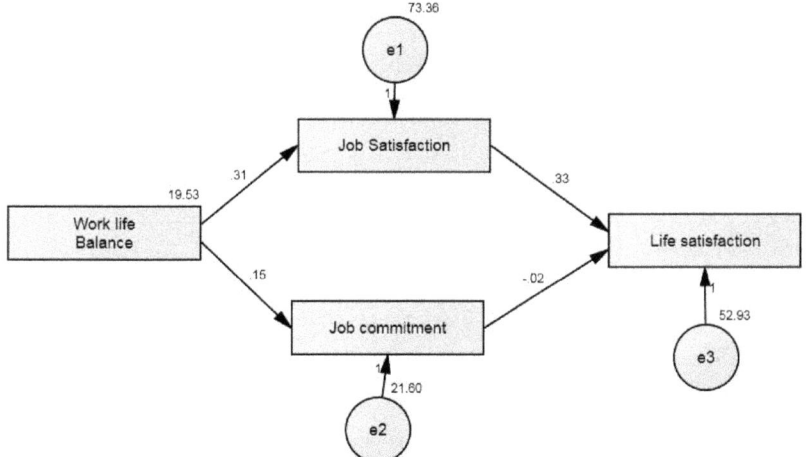

Figure 4.3: Research Model - 3

Model Validity

To ensure the model validity the following indicates are found.

Chi-Square = 124.231, Degree of freedom =2, Proobability=0.000, Goodness of Fit Index (GFI):0.836, Augmented Goodness of Fit(AGFI):0.779, Normative Fit Index NFT):0.774 Relative Fit Index (RFI): 0.771, Incremental Fit Index (IFI):0.779, Comparative Fit Index (CFI): 0.762, Roof Mean Square Error Approximately (RMSEA)=0.089.

All the fit indicates reasonably close to unity (one), and FMSEA closer to Zer0 indicates model validity.

Table 4.40c gives the direct and indirect impact of the constructs under study.

Table 4.40c: Constructs Related

Constructs Related	Direct Effect	Indirect Effect
Work-life balance and Job commitment	0.15(0.154)	0.10(.099)
Work-life balance and Job Satisfaction	0.31(0.308)	
Job commitment and Life Satisfaction	0.02(0.018)	
Job Satisfaction and Life Satisfaction	0.330(0.330)	
Work-life balance and Life Satisfaction		

Source: Primary Data

This analysis reveals that Work-life balance influence Job commitment (15%) and Job satisfaction (31%). Also Work-life balance influence Life satisfaction indirectly through Job satisfaction (33%).

From the above model, it is empirically proved that the Work-life balance of the WCPOs is supported by their superior, Family and Co-worker with Job satisfaction and Job commitment leads to Life satisfaction.

*Organizational
Implications of Work-Life
Conflict*

CHAPTER V

Organizational Implications of Work-Life Conflict

5.1 INTRODUCTION

Human resources which are a part of the service sector is the most significant contributor to the Indian economy. The police profession has a challenging or even outright hostile work environment for women and men officers. Work-life balance is an essential problem in police personal. Work-life balance defines as a fulfillment of role salience between multiple roles, defined work-life balance as 'the extent to which an individual's effectiveness and satisfaction in work and family roles are compatible with the individuals' life role priorities at a given point in time'

Work-Life Balance not only affects the individual but also affects the organisation. Therefore, today solving work-life conflict is the concern for all growing organisations and can be taken as a part of organisation development.

Women continue to carry the significant burden of family and caring responsibilities even though their participation in the workforce is widely accepted. Based on the analysis of the data collected from women civil police officers of Kerala, the study turns up some valuable findings, which are shown under different heads in the following pages.

5.2 OBJECTIVES

1. To assess the opinion on the women civil police officers on the construct that influence work-life balance, family support, the perception of the job, department support, superior support, co-worker support, job commitment, job satisfaction and life satisfaction.

2. To study the interrelationship between work-life balance, family support, the perception of the job, department support, superior support, co-worker support, job commitment, job satisfaction and life satisfaction.

3. To identify the factors that attracted women civil police officers to choose their career in the police.

4. To establish the conceptual model between various antecedents of work-life balance and outcome among women civil police officers.

5.3 FINDINGS

5.3.1 Profile of the Women Civil Police Officers

The summary of the demographic profile of the women civil police officers was listed below:

1. Majority of the WCPOs (49.4%) are in the age group of 31-40, 20.2% WCPO is in the age group of 18-30 and 41- 50 years.

2. About 43.6 % of WCPO have the graduation qualification, followed by post-graduation (21.4%), and pre-degree (19.8%). Only 15.2% of the WCPOs have SSLC qualification.

3. Married WCPOs comprise 87.9%, and WCPO of single status is only 10.5 %.

4. As far as the occupation of a spouse is concerned, 41.6% of spouse having have a government job, 30.7% in private job, 17.9% are businessmen and only 9.7 % work in the same profession.

5. Regarding the type of family, 65.6% of WCPOs live in a nuclear family, and WCPOs of joint family constitute 34.2 %.

6. 89.5% WCPOs family size is three to five members, 6.6 % have up to 2 members and only 3.9 % staying with six or more members.

7. 36.5% of WCPOs do not have the responsibility of adult dependents. However, 25.6%, 20.6% and 17.1% WCPOs have two adults dependent, more than two adult dependent and one adult respectively. 38.5%, 24.5% and 9.4% WCPOs have a responsibility of two, one, and more than two children dependent responsibility. However, 27.62 WCPOs do not have child dependents.

8. About 30.7% of WCPOs have younger children who are above 10 years of age, followed by, 6 to 10 year aged children (27.6%), 19.4% WCOPs have children of 2-5 years of age, 17.1% of WCPOs do not have children and 5% of them have children of under 2 years.

9. About 43.1% of WCPOs have elder children who are above 10 years of age, followed by, 6 to 10-year aged children (27.2%), 12.4 do not have children,

10.5% WCOPs have 2-5 years of age children, 6.6 % WCPOs have children of under 2 years.

10. 56% of WCOPs have one or two male children, followed by 39.3% have no male children, 4.6% have more than two male children.

11. 60.7% WCOPs have one or two female children, followed by 35.4% have no female child. Moreover, 3.9% have more than two female children.

12. Majority of WCPOs (40.5%) spend time with their family only six or seven hours a day. 36.6 % and 22.9% spend less than five hours and more than 7 hours a day.

13. Monthly family income of WCPOs reveals that 65.8 % of the WCPOs earn up to Rs.40,000, 29.6 % of WCPO earn between Rs.40,001 to 60,000 and 4.7 % WCPOs earn between Rs.60,001 to 80,000.

14. 79.4 % of WCPOs stay in their own house. 14.4% used police quarters facility given by the department, remaining 6.2 % stay in the rented house.

15. The majority (50.2%) of the WCPOs are of 11-15 years of service, 20.6 % of the WCPOs have under 6- 10 year of service, 13.2 % WCPO under 16-20 years of service and remaining 16 % WCPO have less than 5 years in service.

16. Of the 62.3% of the WCPOs, 37.7% of WCPO work for six to seven days in a week.

17. Most of the WCPO work (34.2%) in 8 or 9 hours, followed by 32.3% in 10 to 12 hours, 17.9% in 9 or 10 hours and 15.6% 12 hours respectively.

18. In the case of work schedule, 74.3% work in alternative shifts, which mean they work in day shift and night shift in rotation base. 22.6% work in general shift and 3.1% only work in night shifts.

19. 34.6% of WCPO take 1-hour travel to reach their police station, 30.7% require less than half hours, 22.6% need two hours and 12.1% commuter more than two hours.

20. Majority of WCPOs (52.1) are happy about the time spend in their work, 29.2% of WCPOs express a neutral opinion, 11.3% WCPO opine very happy, 6.2% of WCPOs are unhappy and remaining 1.2% of WCPO are dissatisfied.

21. 66.5% WCPOs have not received any award during their service, and 33.5% WCPO has received the award.

22. 50.2% WCPO are satisfied with the infrastructure facility in the department, and 49.8% are not.

5.3.2 Household Responsibilities

The responsibilities of the WCPOs are divided into two; one is household responsibilities and parental responsibilities. Table 4.4 demonstrates on WCPOs time spend on take various household responsibilities for Cooking, cleaning and washing Grocery/ Vegetable purchase, for Shopping, to pay bills (Electricity, water, telephone, banking transactions and therefore, on.), and small household repairs.

Cooking Cleaning and Washing

113 (44%) of WCOPs take 100% responsibilities for the Cooking Cleaning, and washing, followed by 67 (26.1%) take 75% responsibilities, 52 (20.2%) take 50% of work, 15 (5.8%) take 25%, and only 10 (3.9%) do not have any responsibility regarding cooking, cleaning and washing.

Grocery/ Vegetable Purchase

61 (23.7%) of WCOPs take 100% responsibilities for the grocery/vegetables purchase, followed by 60 (23.3%) take 75% responsibilities, 61 (23.7%) take 50% of work, 44 (17.1%) take 25%, and only 31 (12.2%) do not have any responsibility regarding grocery/ vegetable purchase.

Shopping

61 (23.7%) of WCOPs take 100% responsibilities for shopping, followed by 70 (27.2%) take 75% responsibilities, 68 (26.5%) take 50% of work, 45 (17.5%) take 25% , and only 13 (5.1%) do not have any responsibility regarding shopping.

Pay Bills

59 (23%) of WCOPs take 100% responsibilities for bill payment, followed by 52 (20.2%) take 75% responsibilities, 56 (21.8%) take 50% of work, 59 (23 %) take 25%, and only 31 (12 %) do not have any responsibility regarding bill payment.

Small Household Repairs

48 (18.7%) of WCOPs take 100% responsibilities for small household repairs, followed by 43 (16.7%) take 75% responsibilities, 58 (22.6%) take 50% of work, 68 (26.5 %) take 25%, and only 40 (15.5%) do not have any responsibility regarding small household repairs.

5.3.3 Parental Responsibilities

Child Care

90 (35%) of WCPOs take 100% responsibilities for child care, followed by 77 (30.0%) take 75% responsibilities, 42 (16.3%) take 50% of work, 16 (6.2 %) take 25%, and only 4 (1.6 %) do not have any responsibility regarding child care. 28 (10.9%) WCPOs the situation is not applicable.

Helping the Children in their Studies

85 (33.1%) of WCPOs take 100% responsibilities for helping the children in their studies, followed by 48 (18.7%) take 75% responsibilities, 57 (22.2%) take 50% of work, 21 (8.2 %) take 25%, and only 13 (5.1 %) do not have any responsibility regarding helping the children in their studies. 33 (12.8%) WCPOs the situation is not applicable.

Drop and Pick the Children from School/Tuitions/Extracurricular Activities

34 (13.2%) of WCPOs take 100% responsibilities for drop and pick the children from school/tuitions/extracurricular activities, followed by 27 (10.5%) take 75% responsibilities, 55 (21.4%) take 50% of work, 44 (17.1%) take 25%, and only 33 (12.8 %) do not have any responsibility regarding for drop and pick the children from school/tuitions/ extracurricular activities. 64 (24.9%) WCPOs the situation is not applicable.

Take Child Outing

37 (14.4%) of WCPOs take 100% responsibilities for taking child outing, followed by 49 (19.1%) take 75% responsibilities, 68 (26.5%) take 50% of work, 37 (14.4%) take 25%, and only 17 (6.6%) do not have any responsibility regarding child outing. 49 (19.1%) WCPOs the situation is not applicable.

Attend Parent Teacher Meeting

78 (30.4%) of WCPOs take 100% responsibilities for attend parent-teacher meeting, followed by 42 (16.3%) take 75% responsibilities, 62 (24.1%) take 50% of work, 24 (9.3%) take 25%, and only 10 (3.9%) do not have any responsibility regarding attend parent-teacher meeting. 41 (16.0%) WCPOs the situation is not applicable.

Elderly Care

57 (22.2%) of WCPOs take 100% responsibilities for elderly care, followed by 47 (18.3%) take 75% responsibilities, 73 (28.4%) take 50% of work, 34 (13.2%) take 25%, and only 10 (3.9%) do not have any responsibility regarding elderly care. 36 (14%) WCPOs the situation is not applicable.

Financial Support

64 (22.2%) of WCPOs take 100% responsibilities for financial support, followed by 78 (30.4%) take 75% responsibilities, 84 (32.7%) take 50% of work, 17 (6.6%) take 25%, and only 4 (1.6%) do not have any responsibility regarding financial support. 10 (3.9%) WCPOs the situation is not applicable.

Saving and Investment Decision

68 (26.5%) of WCPOs take 100% responsibilities for saving, and investment decision, followed by 63 (24.5%) take 75% responsibilities, 86 (33.5%) take 50% of work, 22 (8.6%) take 25%, and only 5 (1.9%) do not have any responsibility regarding saving and investment decision. 13 (5.1%) WCPOs the situation is not applicable

5.4 FINDINGS BASED ON OBJECTIVES

Objective- I

To assess the opinion on the women civil police officers on the construct the factors influencing work-life balance, family support, the perception of the job, department support, superior support, co-worker support, job commitment, job satisfaction and life satisfaction.

a) **Marital Status and Opinion on Construct**

By the analysis of the study inferred that single and married women civil police officers experience the same level of opinion on the Factors attracting profession,

Work life balance, Family support, Perception of the job, Department support, Co-worker support Job commitment, Job satisfaction and Life satisfaction. However, in the case of superior support, single women civil police officers experience a higher level of superior support.

b) Family type and Opinion on Constructs

The result implies that the women civil police offers living in the joint and nuclear family experience the same level of opinion on Factors attracting profession, Work life balance, Family support, Perception of the job, Department support, Superior support, Co-worker support, Job commitment, Job satisfaction and Life satisfaction.

c) Number of Male Children and Opinion on Constructs

The result shows that all the women police officers who are having one or two male children and not having male children experience the same level of opinion on Factors attracting profession, Work life balance, Family support ,Department support, Superior support, Co-worker support, and Life Satisfaction. But mean value of perception of the job, Job commitment and Job satisfaction indicate that women civil police officers those who have one to two male children experience a higher level of intricacies in the perception of the job, Job commitment and Job satisfaction.

d) Number of Female Child and Opinion on Constructs

The result showed that all the women civil police officers who are having one or female girl children and not having a female child experience the same level of opinion on Department support, Superior support, Coworker Support, Perception of the job, Job commitment, Job satisfaction and Life satisfaction. However, the construct such as Factors attracting profession, Family support, and Work-life balance number of female child dependent care responsibility plays a vital role. Women civil police officers those who have one or two female children experience a higher level of Work-life balance and Family support.

e) Number of days worked in week and Opinion on Constructs

On the basis of the analysis of the study inferred that women civil police officers working six days and seven days in a week experience same level of opinion on Factors attracting profession, Work life balance, Family support, Perception of job, Department support, Superior support, Co-worker support, Job commitment, Job satisfaction and Life satisfaction.

f) Work schedule and Opinion on Constructs

In this study, the opinion given by women civil police officers working in general and alternative shift experience the same level of opinion on Factors attracting profession, Work life balance, Family support, Superior support, Department support, Co-worker support, and Life satisfaction.

However, comparing the mean values, it is concluded that women civil police officers those who are working in general shift experience higher level of support from their department.

g) Award Received and Opinion on Constructs

The study revealed that the entire award received and not received women civil police officers experience the same level of opinion on Factors attracting profession, Perception of the job, Co-worker support and Life satisfaction. However, Work life balance, Family support, Department support, Superior support, Job commitment and Job satisfaction in the case the award received and not received women civil police officers have a significant difference of opinion. Comparing the mean values, it is concluded that women civil police officers those who received award showed a higher level of Family support, Department support, Superior support, Job commitment and Job satisfaction.

h) Infrastructure and Opinion on Constructs

The study showed that all the infrastructure satisfied and dissatisfied women civil police officers experience the same level of opinion on Factors attracting profession, Work life balance, Family support, the perception of the job, Department support, Superior support and Life satisfaction. However, certain cases such as Co-worker support, Job commitment and Job satisfaction, the Infrastructure available is a significant factor, and while Comparing the mean values, it is concluded that women civil police officers those who are satisfied with infrastructure showed a higher level of Co-worker support, Job commitment and Job satisfaction.

i) Zones and Opinion on Constructs

Based on the study all the women civil police officers working under south and north zone experience the same level of opinion on Factors attracting profession, Work life balance, Family support, Department support, Superior support, Co-worker support, the perception of the job, Job commitment and Job satisfaction. But comparing the mean values, it is concluded that women civil police officers those who are working in north zone showed more Life satisfaction.

j) Police station and Opinion on Constructs

On the basis of the study all the women civil police officers working in the local police station and women cell experience the same level of opinion on Factors attracting profession, Work life balance, Family support, the perception of the job, Department support, Superior support, Co-worker support, Job commitment and Job satisfaction and Life satisfaction.

k) Age and Opinion on Constructs

The study emphasises that the women civil police officer belonging to different age group experience the same level of opinion on the constructs Factors attracting profession Work life balance, Family support, Perception of the job, Superior support and Coworker support. However, women civil police officers belonging to different age groups differ in their opinion Department support, Job commitment, Job satisfaction and Life satisfaction. The result of Post Hoc test says that age group 41- 50 is significantly different from 18-30 and 31-40 in the case of job commitment, Job satisfaction and Life satisfaction.

l) Educational Qualification and Opinion on Constructs

As per the study women, civil police officers belonging to the different category of education background shows the same level of opinion on the constructs Factors attracting profession, Work life balance, Perception of the job, Superior support and Life satisfaction. However, women civil police officers belonging to the different category of education background differ in their opinion Family support, Department support, Co-worker support, Job commitment and Job satisfaction.

Post hoc test reveals that women civil police officers belonging to the postgraduate, degree and SSLC. Women civil police officers give a significant opinion on Family support, Department support than the women civil police officers educational group belonging to Pre-degree group. But in the case of Job commitment and Job satisfaction the respondent educational groups S.S.L.C significantly different from 'pre-degree', 'degree' and 'post graduate.'

m) Spouse's Occupation and Opinion on Constructs

According to the result women civil police officers belonging to the different category of spouse's occupation experience the same level of opinion on Work-life balance, Family support, Perception of the job, Co-worker support, Job commitment, Job satisfaction and Life satisfaction.

However, women civil police officers belonging to the different category of spouses occupation differ in their opinion Factors attracting to the profession, Department support and Superior support. The result of Post Hoc test says that spouse's occupation group business is significantly different from the same profession and private in the case of job factors attracting profession. In the case of department support, spouse's occupation group business is significantly different from the same profession. Superior support, spouse's occupation group business is significantly different from a government job.

n) Number of Adult Dependent and Opinion on Constructs

In analysingwomen civil police officers belonging to a different number of adult dependent's group experience the same level of opinion Work life balance, Family support, Perception of the job, Department support, Superior support, Co-worker support, Job commitment, Job satisfaction and Life Satisfaction. Women civil police officers belonging to a different number of adult dependent differ in their opinion Factors attracting to the profession.

o) Number of Child Dependent and Opinion on Constructs

Women civil police officers belonging to a different number of child dependent 's group experience the same level of opinion constructs Factors attracting profession, Work life balance, Family support, Perception of the job, Department support, Superior support, Job commitment, Job satisfaction and Life Satisfaction. However, women civil police officers belonging to a different number of child dependent differ in their opinion on Co-worker Support. The post hoc study mentioned that co-worker support in child dependent concerned; there is a significant difference between single child dependent and no dependent.

p) Income and Opinion on Constructs

The study highlighted that women civil police officers belonging to the different category of income group experience the same level of opinion on Factors attracting profession, Work life balance, Family support, Perception of the job, Superior support. However, women civil police officers belonging to different categories of income group give different level of opinion on Department support, Job commitment, Job satisfaction and Life Satisfaction. The post hoc test identified the income group 40,001 -60,00 and up to 40,000 which are significantly different in their Department support, Job commitment and Life satisfaction.

q) Age of Younger Child and Opinion on Constructs

In analysingwomen civil police officers belonging to a different category or various age group of younger child experience the same level of opinion Factors attracting profession, Family support, Perception of the job, Coworker support, Job commitment, Job satisfaction Life satisfaction.

However, women civil police officers belonging to different age group of a younger child differ in their opinion on Work-life balance Department support and Superior support.

r) Age of Elder Child and Opinion on Constructs

As per the result women civil police officers belonging to the different category of the age group of elder child experience the same level of opinion on Factors attracting profession, Work life balance, Family support, Perception of job Department support, Superior support and Co-worker support. However, in the case of Job Commitment, Job Satisfaction and Life satisfaction.

s) Time spent with family and Opinion on Constructs

By the analysis, it can be inferred that women civil police officers belong to different of hours spend with the family of experience same level of opinion on Work-life balance, Family support, Perception of the job, Superior support, Department support, Job satisfaction and Life satisfaction. However, in certain cases such as Factors attracting to the profession, Co-worker support and Job commitment their opinion is magnitude different.

t) Years of service's Experience and Opinion on Constructs

The result of the study revealed that women civil police officer's different years of service experience give the same level of the opinion the constructs Factors attracting profession, Work life balance, Perception of the job, Superior support, Department support, Coworker support, Job commitment, Job satisfaction and Life satisfaction. However, they showed a different level of opinion on Family support, the perception of the job, co-worker support and Job commitment.

u) Working Hours and Opinion on Constructs

As per the study women, civil police officers belonging to various working hours give the same level of opinion on Factors attracting profession, Work life balance, and Family support, Perception of the job, Superior support, Job commitment, and Life Satisfaction. At the same time, they give different level of opinion on Department support, Coworker support and Job satisfaction.

v) Travelling hours and Opinion on Constructs

Based on the study women civil police officers belonging to various hours spend for travel to workplace experience the same level of opinion on Family support, Department support, Job commitment, and Job and Life Satisfaction. However, in the case of Factors attracting to the profession, Work life balance, the perception of the job, Superior support and Co-worker support their opinion is significantly different.

FINDINGS

Objective-II

To study the interrelationship between work-life balance, family support, the perception of the job, department support, superior support, co-worker support, job commitment, job satisfaction and life satisfaction.

The construct factors attracting profession, Work-life balance, Family support, Perception of the job, Department support, Superior support, Co-worker support, Job commitment, Job Satisfaction on the total Life Satisfaction are related to each other. It was found that by applying the correlation analysis almost all the construct under the study are significantly and positively correlated with each other.

FINDINGS

Objective-III

To identify the factors that attracted women civil police officers to choose their career in the police.

The researcher is interested in finding the items/aspects that attracted the WCPOs to choose this profession. Twelve items were identified for this purpose. However, to find few important items from these items are difficult. Hence, the data reduction method – factor analysis is followed to identify the latent constraints (factors) from these twelve items.

Job consists the first factor is different every day (12), opportunity to help people (2), the prestige of the occupation (11), chance to fight crime (10), excitement about the job (1), a lifetime interest in law enforcement (7) all these statement this factor can be named as **Passion Towards Law Enforcement.**

The second factor is constituted by lack of other job opportunities (8) relative or friends being a police officer (5), the desire to part of a male-dominated occupation (9) this factor can be named as **Manliness.**

The third factor is the combination of security of the job (3) and salary and benefits (4) this factors cab be named as **Job Security.**

Thus it may be concluded that one is **Passion Towards Law Enforcement** second one is **Manliness,** and the third one is **Job Security** are the factors that attract the women civil police officers to this profession.

FINDINGS

Objective-IV

To establish the conceptual model between various antecedents of work-life balance and outcome among women civil police officers.

Model 1 interpreted that Superior support and Coworker Support play a positive and significant role in the Work-life balance of the women civil police officers. Also it worth to note that taking the impact of Superior support, the family also influenced the work-life balance of the women civil police officers. Hence Work-life balance influence positively the Job satisfaction and Life satisfaction of the women civil police officers.

As per the model 11 women, civil police officers experience a good amount of Family support, Co-worker support, Superior support which lead to Work-life balance. Their Work-life balance leads to Job satisfaction and Job commitment. Finally Work life balance, Job satisfaction and Job commitment lead to overall Life satisfaction.

The model developed empirically proved that the Work-life balance of the women civil police officers are supported by their superior, Family and Coworker.The Work-life balance leads to Job Satisfaction and Life Satisfaction.

5.5 SUGGESTIONS

Per se standard and tailor-made approaches are not available to handle issues related to work/life balance. However, based on the findings, informal discussions with women civil police officers and general observations made by the researcher the following suggestions are drawn.

- To develop time management skill, a timetable for every activity in one's life whether professional or personal to be made and followed.

- Prioritizing each activity undertaken helps to take a better decision.

- Finding quality time with family, friends, relatives may well balanced work-life scenario.

- Keeping one's fit would help in all areas thus by minimising chronic illness, absence from work.

- Make a vacation once in a six months or year

- Creating team spirit would bring all to achieve a goal

- Use positive stroke and be empathetic would make a better work environment

- Make a roster to reduce unscheduled working time at maximum

- Increased number of women police would bring their redressal of grievances in a better way of keeping their morale.

- In-service training should include the work-life management technique

- Society should give proper recognition and support to women police officers to fulfil their duty

5.6 CONCLUSION

Work-life balance is increasingly attracting attention at both the national and international levels. In the current scenario, Work Life Balance is considered as an issue of strategic importance to organisations as well as for the employees. There is a number of reasons for its growing importance. Challenges in work-life balance redressed are not only the responsibility of an employer but also these issues can only be resolved by adopting the collective approach. This study is a positive approach that women are making their presence felt in all occupations and particular policing. The responsibilities of the Women Civil Police Officers are divided into two; one is household responsibilities and parental responsibilities. Apart from their life responsibilities which drive the women civil police officers to this profession to take this job is primarily based on **Passion towards Law Enforcement,** followed by **Manliness** and third is **Job Security.**

5.7 IMPLICATIONS FOR FUTURE RESEARCH

- A similar study could be taken considering Male Civil Police Officers

- Studies will be taken by the hierarchy

- Research studies could be taken based on women work in different professions based on their carrier stages and life stages.

Milton Keynes UK
Ingram Content Group UK Ltd.
UKHW020940221123
433051UK00020B/1068